SAYING GOODBYE TO YOUR DEAR D♥G

10 Questions to Help You Decide When It's Time to Euthanize

Written by

DOROTHEA DELEY

Illustrated by

VICKY REES

www.GoodbyeDearDog.com

A DIVISION OF GROWN BY PEOPLE, INC.

Grown by People, Inc.
PO Box 370445
Las Vegas, NV 89137
www.GoodbyeDearDog.com

Copyright © 2021 by Dorothea Deley

All rights reserved. No part of this book may be reproduced in any form or by any electronic or mechanical means, including information storage and retrieval systems, without permission in writing from the publisher, except by a reviewer, who may quote brief passages in a review.

"Kali" Cover Painting by Vicky Rees (www.VickyRees.com)
Cover & Interior Design by Vicky Rees
Illustrations by Vicky Rees
Editing by Charmin Dahl
Photography by Mike Maxwell (unless otherwise credited)

ISBN: 978-0-692-11576-3
Printed in the United States of America

The purpose of this book is to inform and support people facing the euthanasia decision for their dogs. It is sold with the understanding that the publisher is not engaged in rendering psychological, veterinarian, or other professional services. If veterinarian assistance or counseling is needed, please seek the services of a competent professional.

FOR KALI

Forever & Always
My Baby Bups

CONTENTS

Introduction: You Are Not Alone 1
    How to Use this Guidebook 7
    The Icons and What They Mean 8

Section One: Ask Your Vet 11
    QUESTION 1: What is my Dear Dog's prognosis according to our current vet? 13
    QUESTION 2: Do I want my Dear Dog to see a vet specialist? 20

Section Two: Ask Your Dear Dog 29
    QUESTION 3: Is my Dear Dog in physical pain? 31
    QUESTION 4: Does my Dear Dog still enjoy favorite activities? 38
    QUESTION 5: Is my Dear Dog withdrawing socially? 47
    QUESTION 6: Has my Dear Dog's personality or emotional state changed? 52
    QUESTION 7: How is my Dear Dog's quality of life? 60
    QUESTION 8: Has my Dear Dog given me a sign? 70

Section Three: Ask Yourself 79
    QUESTION 9: How is caring for my Dear Dog affecting my family and me? 80
    QUESTION 10: What does my heart tell me to do for my Dear Dog? 89

Section Four: Making Your Decision 95
    Benefits of Deciding to Euthanize 98
    Bringing All 10 Questions Together to Make a Decision 100

Section Five: Once You've Decided 103
    Making the Arrangements — We're Here to Help 105
    End-of-Life Plan for My Dear Dog 117
    Goodbye Dear Kali 119

Section Six: Talking to Your Kids 121
    Explaining Euthanasia to Your Child 124
    Helping Your Child Grieve 125

Section Seven: Resources to Support You 129
    Recommendations for Online Researching 130
    Trusted Veterinary Websites 131
    Ways We Can Support You 132

Conclusion: Thank You & A Gift 135

Acknowledgments 139

> "The bravest among us will always know heartbreak because those are the people who have the courage to love someone."
>
> — Brené Brown

INTRODUCTION:
You Are Not Alone

Kali Made Us a Family

Mike and I had been together for about eight years when we decided to adopt our first Dear Dog. I had been "nesting" for a while, buying dog bowls and blankets. It was time!

At the animal shelter, we split up and wandered the rows of kennels. I knew her the moment I saw her — a skinny Australian cattle dog whose black head didn't match her gray body! She shyly leaned against the wall of her kennel, perhaps for reassurance.

As I approached her, she held my gaze with bright, intelligent eyes.

I knelt down to pet her and she leaned into my hand. Such soft fur! And just like that, I fell in love.

I ran to find Mike. The shelter staff suggested we take her to the play yard. Mike picked up a rope toy, and the moment he cocked back his arm to throw it, this timid dog came alive. She took off running and in an instant returned with the toy. She dropped it at Mike's feet, and as he leaned down to pick it up she snatched it up again! (Little did we know this would be an ongoing battle of theirs for years to come!)

After we signed the adoption papers, we loaded her up in the covered bed of our pickup. Before we were even out of the parking lot, though, she had squeezed herself through the cab window and onto my lap.

I was finally a Dog Mom.

We named our girl Kali. Overnight, she transformed us from a couple to a family. We loved her with all our hearts.

We're Here to Support You

Fifteen years later Kali's health declined, and we decided it was time to euthanize her. Or rather, Mike and I *struggled* to decide. It was by far the hardest decision we had ever made.

While we both had dogs as kids, neither of us had been through this process before as adults — the ones making the decision. We felt scared, alone, and confused. We didn't know what to do. We didn't know where to turn.

We don't want you to feel that way with your Dear Dog, so we created this guidebook to help you through this difficult time.

Our hope is that this guidebook helps you decide when to say goodbye to your Dear Dog with love and clarity.

Mike and I, and all the Dog Parents who share their stories within these pages, are here to support you.

"We named our girl Kali. Overnight, she transformed us from a couple to a family. We loved her with all our hearts."

— *Dorothea Deley, Kali's Mom*

10 Questions To Guide You

Euthanasia may be on your mind right now for several reasons. Your Dear Dog may be:

- ♥ Showing signs of age like playing less and sleeping more.
- ♥ Disengaging from life and withdrawing from you.
- ♥ Suffering from a progressively debilitating chronic condition like arthritis, kidney disease or congestive heart failure.
- ♥ Deteriorating rapidly from a terminal disease like inoperable cancer.

You want to make the most loving choice for your fur baby when the time comes, but how do you know?

Mike and I spent months reflecting on our experience with Kali: What did we do right? What do we wish we had done better?

We asked other Dog Parents the same questions, and noticed recurring themes. That gave us the idea for 10 Questions — ones we all agreed would have helped us decide.

The 10 Questions Are:

1. What is my Dear Dog's prognosis according to our current vet?
2. Do I want my Dear Dog to see a vet specialist?
3. Is my Dear Dog in physical pain?
4. Does my Dear Dog still enjoy favorite activities?
5. Is my Dear Dog withdrawing socially?
6. Has my Dear Dog's personality or emotional state changed?
7. How is my Dear Dog's quality of life?
8. Has my Dear Dog given me a sign?
9. How is caring for my Dear Dog affecting my family and me?
10. What does my heart tell me to do for my Dear Dog?

Each question comes with a guide sheet for you to fill out to help you answer it. Fill them out in order or skip around — it's up to you. The guide sheet on page 100 brings all 10 questions together in one place.

Your Heart Is Bigger Than Your Hurt

As dog owners, we're responsible for our dog's health and happiness. This responsibility is part of the "contract" we sign with love the day we adopt our best friends.

It is that very love that moves us to end our Dear Dog's suffering when the time comes.

This is the tragic paradox of being a Dog Parent.

Love tells us that it is better to endure the pain of a broken heart than let our dogs suffer the pain of a broken body.

That is why we say your heart is bigger than your hurt. And your heart will guide you.

Any time you lose your way emotionally or feel overwhelmed, take a moment, place a hand over your heart, and say:

> *"When I listen to my heart, I do good things.*
> *My heart is bigger than my hurt."*

Consider this phrase a comforting mantra — a gift you give yourself when you need courage to continue.

We'll remind you about the mantra throughout the guidebook with the "Say Mantra" box above.

Now it's time to give yourself permission.

SAY MANTRA

Put your hands over your heart and say aloud:

"When I listen to my heart, I do good things."

"My heart is bigger than my hurt."

> "When a pet is suffering and we cannot help anymore, then I think euthanasia is an act of love. Still very hard for the owners, and hard for the doctor as well. But it can be a final act of love."
>
> — *Dr. Steve Colter, Retired Veterinarian*

FILL OUT
My Permission Slip below

WEBSITE:
GoodbyeDearDog.com/
guidesheets

Giving Yourself Permission

There is no absolute "right" or "wrong" time to euthanize your Dear Dog. There is only the "best" time for you, your family, and your pet.

Determining that best time depends on many factors we'll explore together in this guidebook. You may choose something different than other Dog Parents in the book. That's okay. This is about what's best for you and your fur baby.

What I hope you can give yourself now is what I wish I would have given myself when deciding about Kali: Permission.

- ♥ Permission to make a decision.
- ♥ Permission to trust yourself and your decision.
- ♥ Permission to act on your decision.
- ♥ Permission to give your dog a peaceful passing, when it's time.

HERE IS A PERMISSION SLIP FOR YOU TO FILL OUT.

Whenever you lose your way, get scared or feel overwhelmed, pull it out and re-read it.

My Permission Slip

I, _____, love my Dear Dog _____ very much. I know that she/he loves me very much too.

My dog is counting on me to end his/her life peacefully and humanely when the right time comes. The right time is a combination of what is best for my pup and what is best for our family and me. I will do the best I can.

I give myself permission to:

- make this difficult decision with love and compassion for myself and my dog;
- choose a peaceful death for my dog;
- trust my decision; and
- act on my decision in a timely manner.

_____ _____
Your Signature   Today's Date

How To Use This Guidebook

There is no right or wrong way to read this book — do what feels right to you. Here are a few possibilities:

1. Read the entire book and fill out all the guide sheets.
2. Read the entire book and fill out only the applicable guide sheets.
3. Skip to the questions that fit your dog's situation and fill out those guide sheets.
4. Skim the book and skip the guide sheets.
5. Jump to page 100 for all the guide sheet questions on one page. Answer the ones you can, and for those you can't, read those question chapters.

Don't feel like you have to answer all 10 Questions. Then again, I encourage you to answer the questions you don't want to — sometimes the ones we resist are the very ones we need to look at.

Unless your Dear Dog is in pain and your veterinarian is suggesting euthanasia now, you have time to make your decision.

Why the Guide Sheets Help

Open-ended questions like "How's my dog feeling?" leave us vulnerable to seeing what we want to see. Concrete questions, like, "How's my dog's appetite?" work better. They take the guesswork — and the wishful thinking — out of the equation.

That's what the guide sheets are designed to do. Filling them out helps you collect information about your dog's health and happiness and reflect objectively on it.

We compiled all the guide sheets from this guidebook into one PDF. Go to **GoodbyeDearDog.com/ guidesheets** to download the printer-friendly packet.

GET SUPPORT

Download packet of all guide sheets

WEBSITE:
GoodbyeDearDog.com/
guidesheets

"It's helpful for dog owners to write down what they are thinking."

— *Teresa Petterson, DVM*

The Icons and What They Mean

As you work through this book, look for these icons so you know what action we want you to take:

Supplemental Material Online

Everything you need to make your decision is in this guidebook. Supplemental (not required) material is also available at no cost on our website, GoodbyeDearDog.com, such as:

- ♥ printer-friendly versions of the guide sheets
- ♥ resources like Dog Parent interview videos
- ♥ links to veterinary articles and sites we recommend

Throughout the book you'll see icons pointing you to the optional online material.

Make A Dear Dog Binder

You'll want to keep everything related to your doggo's health all in one place. This is such a kindness to yourself! We suggest making a 3-ring binder for the guide sheets, dog's medical records, notes from your vet appointments, and anything else you'd like to include. Create your own or purchase our Dear Dog binder at the link in the "Get Support" box. Start your binder now — it's helpful even when your dog is healthy.

When To Use Your Dear Dog Binder

Here are several ways your Dear Dog binder will come in handy:

VET APPOINTMENTS
- ♥ Keep your thoughts organized.
- ♥ Get your questions answered.
- ♥ Store everything in one place so it's easy to grab-and-go.

FAMILY DISCUSSIONS
- ♥ Hear other perspectives on your pooch's situation.
- ♥ Discuss options if others are involved in decision-making.
- ♥ Get support.

REASSURANCE AFTERWARD
- ♥ Counter any regret or doubt you may feel in the future.
- ♥ Remind yourself why you did what you did.
- ♥ Affirm you made the right decision.

> **GET SUPPORT**
>
> Make or Buy a Dear Dog Binder
>
> **WEBSITE:**
> *GoodbyeDearDog.com/support*

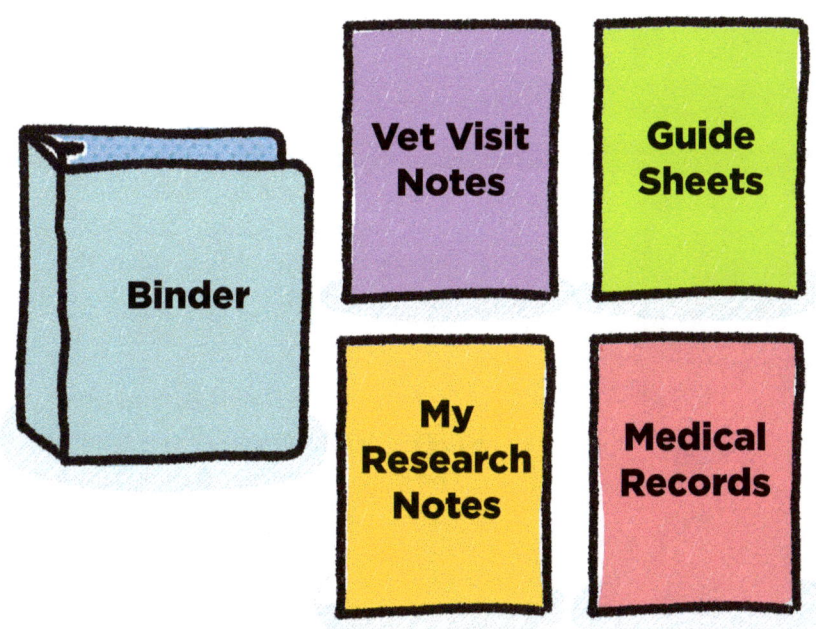

KALI'S STORY

Kali Was More Than A Dog to Me

Kali was such a character! When she wanted me to wake up, she'd scratch my side of the bed. When she wanted to go for a walk, she'd grab her leash and drag it all over the house. When she wanted to eat, she'd scratch the refrigerator door.

My favorite, though, was when she wanted a toy. She'd sit in front of the high shelf where we kept her toy basket and yip!

"This one?" I'd ask, taking down one of her toys.

Kali would sniff it, take it into her mouth, and drop it as if to say, "Nope! Not this one."

Then she'd look back up at the toy basket and yip again. We'd repeat this little game until finally I gave her the toy she wanted. (It was always the horse in a trench coat smoking a cigar! I knew that and would purposely give it to her last. Ha ha! Kali made me laugh. A lot!)

The Kali-Shaped Hole in my Heart

Kali was more than an entertaining character, though. She was also my best friend.

Each day while I wrote whatever project I was working on at the time, Kali would lay by my side. She'd listen while I rehearsed my speeches, looking at me intently so I could practice my "eye contact."

When I was sick on the living room couch, she'd check on me throughout the night, nuzzling me with her nose so I'd know she was there.

In my darkest moments she was there to comfort me, like the time I got a call that my dear friend had drowned. When I collapsed to the floor, Kali let me hug her and sob into her soft fur.

Having Kali in my life truly felt like having another person around.

Now that she's gone there's a Kali-shaped hole in my heart. But, my heart has healed around that hole, sealing Kali inside forever.

It's been five years since Kali died and my love for her remains. My favorite memories of our time together remain. My joy for having known her remains. What a gift it is to love a dog! We Dog Parents are the luckiest people around. ♥

SECTION ONE:
Ask Your Vet

"Your veterinarian cannot make this decision for you but can help you to understand what the future might hold..."

— *Dr. Leslie Sinclair, DVM, Ask the Vet about Dogs*

Adobe Stock Image

Vets Care — Work With One You Trust

Veterinarians become vets because they love animals and want them to live happy, healthy lives. Most of them are dedicated, caring professionals.

A vet can help you understand how much pain your dog might be in, how your dog's disease will likely play out, and what symptoms to watch for.

They can offer treatment options in some cases, or hospice and pain management in others. And at the end, they will be there for you and your Dear Dog when you choose euthanasia.

What your vet cannot do, though, is make that difficult decision for you.

They can only guide you and answer your questions. That's why it's so important to work with a qualified veterinarian you trust.

If the vet already knows your Dear Dog, that's even better. But the most important thing is that YOU feel comfortable with the vet.

Many common diseases progress in fairly predictable stages — although no two dogs will progress in the exact same way or at the exact same rate. For you and your dog, though, going through this for the first time, it will be all new.

That's how it felt for Mike and me with Kali. We were in unknown territory with her congestive heart failure.

A competent vet can guide you through the stages so you know what symptoms to look for and what to expect.

Now let's explore ways to talk to your vet.

QUESTION

What is my Dear Dog's prognosis according to our current vet?

THE STORY OF DASH

Danielle Kemper had been fostering dogs in western Colorado for almost a year when a friend called about an impossible case — a feral border collie rescued out of a Dumpster. "He probably fell in looking for food," she had said.

Photo by Vendia Stockdale

Danielle named the dog "Dash" because he was hard to catch. Months later he'd still run off whenever he had the chance! Over time, "Dash carefully, slowly, painfully began to trust me," Danielle says. Too slowly to be adopted anywhere else but with her though, and so she kept him.

Dash excelled at obedience training and surprised Danielle with an affectionate personality. He followed her everywhere like a shadow and together they trained for half-marathons, rode horses on nearby trails, hiked the hills above their property, and traveled to Mexico.

"He was my sweet, impossible, feral-at-heart collie," Danielle says.

A few years later, Dash was diagnosed with bone cancer. Danielle's wonderful friend and vet broke the news to her — Dash had a tumor on his skull near his eye. It was aggressive and incredibly painful. Gently the vet explained Dash only had 30 to 60 days to live.

For the next month Danielle would catch herself thinking, "By fall, I will not have Dash."

Their remaining time together flew by. Even when Dash could no longer open his mouth wide enough to hold a tennis ball, he still wanted to play fetch. He couldn't yawn anymore, and yet, there he was, still wanting to ride in the pickup truck or go swimming. Still wanting to eat cheese or be petted.

Too soon, the time came for Dash to make his final dash. The vet came to Danielle's ranch. Out on the grassy lawn where Dash loved playing fetch, the vet relieved Dash of his suffering. She and Danielle shared a quiet moment as a dragonfly landed on Dash's white fur, and then flew away. They knew Dash was free now.

"My vet friend is wise and kind beyond measure," says Danielle.

READ MORE

Danielle Shares Dash's Story

WEBSITE: GoodbyeDearDog.com/ resources

ASK VET

Take Guide Sheet #1 (page 17) to your next vet appointment.

Preparing to Talk to Your Vet

Here are a few suggestions for getting the most out of your vet appointments:

1. *Prepare a list of questions beforehand on Guide Sheet #1.*

After the difficult experience I had with our new vet I created a questionnaire for you to use with your vet — questions I wish I would have asked. They're direct and will help you understand what's happening with your Dear Dog, what the future might bring, and how to prepare. See Guide Sheet #1: "Questions to Ask the Vet When My Dear Dog is Sick," on page 17.

2. *Take notes during your vet appointment.*

Sometimes vets throw a lot of info our way rapidly. It's overwhelming. Writing it down helps. You'll be able to review the information later when you get home, where it'll be easier to process. Plus, you can discuss your notes with family members or friends.

3. *Be direct and ask for clarification.*

Tell your vet what you want to know, and ask for clarification if you need. Don't be afraid to ask the same questions over and over again. Your Dear Dog's life is in your hands, and it's important to understand what is happening. If the vet is busy, ask to talk to a vet tech instead.

4. *Ask about euthanasia options now.*

I know it doesn't feel right asking about euthanasia now. It seems premature and feels like betraying your best friend. Look at this way: All you're doing is collecting information. That way, when the time does come, you'll know what to do next. Otherwise you'll be scrambling to make arrangements when you're overwhelmed and distraught. Please don't put yourself through that. We suggest having an end-of-life plan in place now. Knowing who will do the euthanasia and where will it take place provides peace of mind. (See Guide Sheet #1, question 5 on page 17. You can also jump to Guide Sheet #13 on page 117.)

BRINGING A FRIEND HELPS

Because of Mike's crazy work schedule, I had been handling Kali's vet care myself. As her condition worsened I felt like I was failing as a Dog Mom. I couldn't explain to Mike what the vet had said because I didn't understand or couldn't remember.

Thankfully, I finally asked Mike to go with us to our next vet appointment. He and the vet seemed to have a better rapport. Plus Mike wasn't afraid to ask questions.

It made such a difference to have him there! I wish I had asked him sooner.

5. Bring along a trusted friend or family member.

Having another set of ears listening for you is invaluable. Your friend or family member can ask for clarification, take notes, make sure you ask all your questions, and offer moral support. This allows you to focus on the discussion with your vet. They can also debrief with you afterward.

6. Get copies of lab reports and test results.

Ask the vet tech or receptionist for copies of your dog's records, including recent lab reports and test results. Put them in your Dear Dog binder (see page 9). You'll need them later.

Not Sure How to Start the Conversation?

Vets want what's best for your pet. If you're unsure how to broach Guide Sheet #1 with your vet, just say, "I'm really worried about my dog right now and feel a little overwhelmed. I brought a list of questions to help me understand what's going on and what our options are. If you're too busy to talk right now, could I make another appointment with you or talk to the vet tech today?"

Photo by Michelle Brunson

Gustavo Brett chose euthanasia for his 7-year-old dog Sidney when he found out she had inoperable cancer. Their generous vet had been with them from the beginning, when Gustavo first adopted Sidney. And he was there with them at the end, too. Sidney died peacefully outside surrounded by friends and family.

WATCH THIS

Gustavo Shares Sidney's Story

WEBSITE: *GoodbyeDearDog.com/videos*

FILL OUT

Questions to Ask the Vet on next page

WEBSITE:
GoodbyeDearDog.com/ guidesheets

After Your Vet Appointment

After your vet visit, answer the following questions:

1. Did the vet or staff give me adequate information?
   ☐ Yes   ☐ No

2. Did the vet or staff spend enough time answering my questions?
   ☐ Yes   ☐ No

3. Did the vet or staff take me and my concerns seriously?
   ☐ Yes   ☐ No

If you answered "no" to any of the three questions above, feel free to find another vet. You and your kiddo deserve kind veterinary service and patient communication now more than ever.

Mike and I made the mistake of sticking with a vet we didn't understand or trust. If you'd like to read more, see "5 Things We Wish We'd Done Differently Before Euthanizing Kali" at GoodbyeDearDog.com/resources.

TAKE A BREAK

Spend some time with your Dear Dog for a cuddle session or play date!

Take Your Fur Baby on a Doggie Date!

That may have been an intense vet appointment for you! That's a lot of questions to ask and a lot of answers to ponder. It's time to do something nice for yourself and your Dear Dog — a Doggie Date!

What does your dog love to do that the two of you could do immediately after your vet appointment? Here are some fun ideas:

♥ Walk at a nearby park or trail.
♥ Relax at a dog-friendly café with coffee for you and a treat for your pup.
♥ Visit a dog park and let your furbaby run around with friends.
♥ Go to a pet store and let your dog pick out a treat or toy.
♥ Drive around for awhile with the windows cracked open.

If your dog's health is an issue, is there a way you can adapt the date?

Think about what your special guy or gal loves to do, and go do it!

GUIDE SHEET #1

DOG'S NAME: _____ TODAY'S DATE: _____

Questions to Ask the Vet When My Dear Dog is Sick

INSTRUCTIONS: Take this guide sheet to your next vet appointment. (If you've already been to the vet and gotten a diagnosis, fill this out based on that visit.) Read through it beforehand and highlight the questions you'd like to ask. Add your own at the end. Then write in your vet's responses in the space provided, and put in your Dear Dog binder.

1. **Does my dog have a diagnosis?**

   ☐ **YES, we have a diagnosis:**

   a. What is it? _____
   _____

   b. How does this condition/disease usually progress?_____
   _____

   c. Are there predictable stages? If so, which stage is my dog in?_____
   _____

   d. What is my dog's prognosis? What will the future likely hold?_____
   _____

   ☐ **NO, we don't have a diagnosis:**

   a. Do you need to do more tests to diagnose my dog's condition? _____
   _____

   b. What are they and how much will they cost?_____
   _____

2. **Are treatment options available?**

   ☐ **YES, treatments are available:** ☐ **NO, treatments are not available.**

   a. What are they?_____
   _____

   b. Are they painful?_____
   _____

   c. What are their side effects? Will they make my dog feel worse? _____
   _____

   d. How much will they cost? _____
   _____

   continued on next page

©2020 Dorothea Deley. www.GoodbyeDearDog.com

GUIDE SHEET #1 (Continued)

3. **What will likely happen if we do nothing at all?**
   _____
   _____
   _____

4. **How will I know if my dog is suffering?**
   _____
   _____
   _____

5. **For future reference, could we discuss end-of-life options now?**

   a. When would you recommend euthanasia? _____
      _____

   b. What is your euthanasia process? _____
      _____

   c. Do you make euthanasia house calls?   ☐ Yes   ☐ No
      If not, can you recommend a vet who provides in-home euthanasia? _____
      _____

   d. What is the cost of your euthanasia services?
      i. In-clinic euthanasia = $ _____
      ii. At-home euthanasia = $ _____

   e. Do you provide cremation services?   ☐ Yes   ☐ No
      If not, or if I decide to take my dog myself, where do you recommend? _____
      _____

   f. What is the cost of your cremation services?
      i. Group = $ _____
      ii. Individual = $ _____

   g. Are there additional services or charges, such as crematory pick-up costs? _____
      _____

6. **Other questions I have:**
   _____
   _____
   _____
   _____

©2020 Dorothea Deley. www.GoodbyeDearDog.com

KALI'S STORY

Struggling with A New Vet, Missing Our Old Vets

We had just moved to a big city in a new state when Kali's abdomen started to swell. Since we didn't have a new vet yet, I picked the nearest one.

How I wish we could have worked with our Colorado vets instead! They had known Kali for years and we trusted them implicitly. They were down-to-earth docs in their cowboy boots and hiking boots. When they laid out the facts, they didn't sugarcoat them. They explained the options clearly and I knew where we stood.

Our new city vet, in his crisp white lab coat, spoke in medical jargon a mile a minute. He handed me a list of tests with their costs — and like ordering from a restaurant menu, I was supposed to choose Kali's care. I felt overwhelmed, confused, and terrified I would choose wrong.

Eventually he diagnosed Kali with congestive heart failure. Her poor heart had been working so hard it had doubled in size! One of her heart valves couldn't close properly and was leaking lymph and other fluid into her abdomen.

Her prognosis was poor. But our new vet didn't tell us that — or at least I don't recall him saying that. I was lost in all his medicalese.

Doubting the Vet Meant Doubting Myself

Not understanding how near the end we were, Mike and I naively thought we could prolong — improve even — Kali's life with medication and veterinary care. But the meds for her heart failure exacerbated her pre-existing kidney disease. The side effects made her nauseous, exhausted, and dizzy. Kali was miserable.

Worst of all, she had to go in every other week for a "belly tap" to drain off the fluid from her abdomen through a thick needle.

One afternoon when I picked Kali up, the vet handed me a disturbing photo of two plastic buckets filled with a pinkish liquid. "We drained two liters from her abdomen this time," he said. I felt sick to my stomach.

The vet tech gently petted Kali between the ears. "It's pretty uncomfortable when there's that much fluid," she said. "I rub her forehead right here to try and keep her calm during the procedure."

We stood there awkwardly for a moment. Finally, the vet said, "I don't know how many more of these procedures she can take."

At the time it felt like they were speaking in secret code to me. Only now, in retrospect, do I see they were trying to tell me it was time to let Kali go.

QUESTION 2

Do I want my Dear Dog to see a vet specialist?

THE STORY OF PACO

Charmin Dahl wanted to adopt a pal for her older gal, "Dolly Parton the Wonder Beagle." At the animal shelter, she and her partner found the perfect dog — an overweight senior Beagle with a torn up ear.

"They thought maybe he had been living on the streets," Charmin says. "Or maybe with a backyard breeder. He definitely didn't know how to be a dog!"

Charmin and Allison named him Paco and slimmed him down to a healthy size. He and Dolly were happy together.

Photo by Charmin Dahl

Several years later Paco suddenly lost a ton of weight. He started drinking lots of water. Charmin took him to their vet Dr. Bob, who thought Paco might have pancreatitis. Dr. Bob referred them to a veterinarian specialist.

"In my gut I knew Paco couldn't be cured," Charmin says. "It was more about giving him a good quality of life at the end."

Charmin and Allison told the vet specialist they wanted to confirm their primary vet's diagnosis. "We said if this is a lost cause we'll just take Paco home and enjoy our time with him. But the vet specialist said, no, let's see what we can do."

Charmin describes what happened next as trial and error treatment.

"We'd try one medication and the specialist would say come back in two weeks and we'll see how Paco's doing." When that medication didn't work, the specialist would try another one to see if Paco responded to it.

This went on for several months until Charmin took Paco back to their primary vet. "By then Paco was so sickly, so skinny and wasted. I told Dr. Bob we've been doing this for several months and it's not working."

Dr. Bob agreed and they decided to put Paco down.

"I felt like we got a lot more time with Paco," says Charmin, "several months more. But I think we ended up doing that more for us than for him."

Benefits of Seeing a Vet Specialist

Your primary vet may refer you to a specialist if they believe it might help your dog. Sometimes diagnostic tests are needed that they do not have the equipment to provide or expertise to interpret. Other times treatment protocols are needed that they do not provide.

Or you may decide to see a specialist on your own without a referral. A specialist can:

Confirm Your Primary Vet's Diagnosis

You may feel the need for another vet's opinion for whatever reason. Confirming a diagnosis may also help you accept it — especially if it's terminal.

> "I'm a huge fan of second opinions. And I tend to like them courtesy of specialists. While specialists might not always offer you the best bedside manner, and other second-opinion vets might not know you well, getting one more brain on the job… might help nudge you in the right direction… or it might just save your pet's life."
>
> — Dr. Patty Khuly, PetMD.com, Veterinarian

Verify Your Primary Vet's Treatment Plan

You may want to verify that your vet's recommended treatment plan is the best course of action for your pup.

Provide Specialized Treatment such as Chemotherapy

When your dog requires treatment that your primary vet does not provide, seeing a specialist experienced in your dog's illness makes sense.

Handle Emergency Medical Care

When you rush your dog to an emergency veterinary hospital, you may see a vet who is specially trained in emergency and critical care.

Offer End-of-Life Care

Hospice veterinarians specialize in end-of-life care for pets. They can:

- ♥ help you understand your Dear Dog's declining health,
- ♥ manage her pain,
- ♥ keep her comfortable, and
- ♥ help you decide when it's time to say goodbye.

Search online for a vet in your area that provides hospice services for pet. You might also check Lap of Love Veterinary Hospice's directory to see if one of their mobile veterinarians works in your area. Or contact the veterinary college at your local university for compassionate end-of-life support and services.

Grant Yourself Peace of Mind

A nagging doubt in the back of your mind may be reason enough to seek out a specialist. Knowing you did everything you could have can give you invaluable peace of mind — especially later on.

> "The specialist's expertise complements that of your veterinarian. You may be referred to a veterinary specialist if diagnosing or treating your pet's health problem requires specialized equipment and/or expertise that your veterinarian does not have."
>
> — *American Veterinary Medical Association (avma.org)*

When our new vet diagnosed Kali with congestive heart failure, I wish I had taken her to see a cardiology specialist. I didn't doubt his diagnosis. I doubted his treatment plan. And because I had that doubt but didn't explore other options, I'm haunted to this day by that decision.

I know even a vet cardiologist wouldn't have been able to "save" Kali. But I wonder — could they have given her a more comfortable final few months?

Seeing a Specialist Gave Zorro Extra Time

My sister's Doberman Zorro loved the beach! Before he got sick, he and his cousin Jenna took a California vacation (with their moms, of course). During the day they chased each other on the beach. At night they curled up together on the hotel bed.

When Zorro started limping, my sister took him to her primary vet for a check-up. The diagnosis wasn't good — osteosarcoma (bone cancer) in one of his back legs. The vet referred them to an oncologist, a specialist trained to treat cancers.

After wrestling with the excruciating treatment options, my sister chose amputation. During Zorro's treatment, the oncologist kept her primary vet in the loop and they coordinated his care and recovery.

Zorro lived another six months and my sister is grateful they had that extra time together. They even took several more trips to Zorro's favorite beach!

Risks of Seeing a Vet Specialist

Many of the Dog Parents we interviewed chose not to pursue a second opinion from a vet specialist for a variety of reasons. Sometimes working with a specialist can:

Keep You in a Treatment Loop

Working with a vet specialist may involve lots of vet visits plus trial-and-error treatments and medications. This can be hard on your dog — and you.

Cost More than You Can Afford

Veterinary specialists usually cost more than general vets. Before we left Colorado, our vet thought Kali might have a heart murmur and referred us to a cardiologist. The initial exam with tests would have cost us $1,000 — money we didn't have at the time.

Only you know what you can reasonably afford on specialist care. Keep in mind you might spend the money and still be unable to save your dog.

Prolong Suffering

Even if a veterinary specialist cannot save your dog, they may be able to buy you some extra time with your fur baby. But, is that extra time worth it if your pup is miserable?

Before you make an appointment with a specialist, ask yourself these questions:

- ♥ At what point is my dog's quality of life too compromised — from the illness or the medication's side effects?
- ♥ Is my pooch happy, or at the very least, comfortable enough right now without specialized treatment?
- ♥ If a specialist can buy us extra time together, is that time for my dog — or for me?

You might discuss the above questions with your primary vet, too.

> "We took our dog Paco to a specialist to get a confirmed diagnosis. I'm glad we did that — we got a lot more time with Paco. But then what happened was a long period of 'trial and error' treatment that ultimately left him wasted and sickly."
>
> — *Charmin Dahl, Paco's Mom*

What's the Difference between a Primary Vet and a Specialist Vet?

If you're not sure what the difference is between "generalist" veterinarians and their "specialist" counterparts, don't worry. I wasn't either! So I put together this chart based on information from the American Veterinary Medical Association (AVMA):

	GENERALIST VET	SPECIALIST VET
EDUCATION	4-year doctorate degree in veterinary medicine that combines classroom instruction with experience in the laboratory and vet clinic setting.	4-year doctorate degree in veterinary medicine that combines classroom instruction with experience in the laboratory and vet clinic setting. Additional training in a specialty area that often includes a residency in a clinical setting.
LICENSING	Must pass state licensing requirements to practice veterinary medicine.	Must pass state licensing requirements to practice veterinary medicine.
AREAS OF EXPERTISE	Like your family physician, a general practice veterinarian treats a broad variety of health conditions, and has experience with both acute and chronic illnesses. They can: • perform some surgeries • spay and neuter • conduct dental cleanings/extractions • provide euthanization services • guide you in general care of your dog A vet generalist's goal is to work with you — and veterinary specialists as needed — to keep your pet healthy.	Specialist vets narrow their focus to a particular type of animal (i.e., reptiles) or specific area of the body (i.e., joints.) The AVMA recognizes 22 areas of veterinary specialty, including: • Dentistry • Dermatology • Emergency/Critical Care • Internal Medicine • Cardiology • Neurology • Oncology • Microbiology • Nutrition • Ophthalmology • Pathology • Radiology • Sports Medicine & Rehabilitation • Surgery • Surgery – Orthopedics • Surgery – Soft Tissue • Toxicology

	GENERALIST VET	**SPECIALIST VET**
RELATIONSHIP WITH YOU	Already has an established relationship with you and your dog.	Has no history or established relationship with you or your dog.
COST	Varies depending on your location.	Varies depending on your location and specialist area; more costly than a general vet.
HOW TO FIND ONE	You're on your own to find a vet, either through recommendations from friends or online reviews. More than likely your current vet is a generalist. You can ask them if you're not sure.	Your primary vet refers you to a specialist most often (although you can seek one out on your own). Some veterinary practices have both generalist and specialist vets; in that case you'd be referred to a specialist in the same clinic as your primary vet.
COLLABORATION	A generalist vet will refer you to a specialist if your dog's condition requires diagnostic equipment or expertise your vet does not have. Sometimes they have a specialist interpret test results and consult on a treatment plan for your dog. Your primary vet will then work closely with the vet specialist in treating your dog. It's important both your primary and specialist veterinarians communicate with each other and you to make sure your pup receives the best care.	A vet specialist's expertise complements your primary veterinarian. While they may have extensive experience treating your dog's health issue, they will rely on your primary vet for a medical history, test results, and ongoing assessments. It's important both your primary and specialist veterinarians communicate with each other and you to make sure your pup receives the best care.

FILL OUT

Questions to Ask Vet Specialist on next page

WEBSITE:
GoodbyeDearDog.com/guidesheets

Do the Best You Can

The decision to see a veterinary specialist or not can be a tough one for some of us. Just know there's no right or wrong decision. We all do the best we can with the resources and information we have at the time.

If you do decide to see a specialist, the guide sheet on the next page will help you know what to ask at your first appointment.

Adobe Stock Image

"I trusted my vet, so later when my dog Amelia was sick I didn't feel the need to get a second opinion from a specialist."

— *Jan Simmons, Amelia's Mom*

GUIDE SHEET #2

DOG'S NAME: _____ TODAY'S DATE: _____

Questions to Ask a Vet Specialist

INSTRUCTIONS: Call the vet specialist's office to make an appointment. Explain your primary vet referred you if that's the case. Ask if they can request records from your primary vet, or if you need to get copies to bring to your appointment. (Some records can be sent electronically.) If you filled out Guide Sheet #1 (page 17), bring it and this guide sheet to discuss with the vet specialist. Write down any specific questions you have beforehand in #6 below.

1. **My primary vet diagnosed my dog with this condition:** _____

2. **I would like a second opinion. What is your preliminary diagnosis?** _____

3. **What tests would you need to do to confirm the diagnosis?** _____

    a. How much will those tests cost? _____

4. **How does this condition usually progress? Are there predictable stages, and if so, which stage is my dog in?** _____

5. **Can my dog's illness be treated or managed? If so:**

    a. What are the treatments and/or medications? _____

    b. Are the treatments painful? _____

    c. Are there side effects to the medication that will compromise my dog's quality of life? _____

    d. How much will the treatments and/or medications cost? _____

    e. How much time do you think the treatments/medications may buy us? _____

6. **Other questions I have:** _____

7. **I want you to:**

    ☐ treat my dog   ☐ work with my primary vet   ☐ let me think about it and get back to you

©2020 Dorothea Deley. www.GoodbyeDearDog.com

KALI'S STORY

Vet Specialists Saved Young Kali's Life

When Kali was 7 years old, we moved to a little ranching community in the mountains of western Colorado. The day we moved in, Kali kept throwing her ball at our feet while we tried to unload the U-Haul.

Mike wanted to keep her entertained (and not underfoot!) so he kicked the ball. Off Kali went, 90 miles an hour after her toy. She stopped suddenly in the alfalfa field beyond our farmhouse. She looked down at her leg, and then up at us. Something was wrong.

We ran to her and stopped short. Kali had flayed open the inside of her back left leg on an irrigation pipe jutting out of the ground. The wound was gruesome. Mike and I were terrified.

We wrapped her in a towel and drove to the only vet clinic in town. There we met the country vet Doc Chuck. Generous, practical, and low tech, he ran a one-man operation.

Doc Chuck gave Kali a pain shot and crated her in the back room until he could operate later that evening.

For the next five weeks Kali's leg wouldn't stop bleeding through the stapled stitches. Doc Chuck kept giving her vitamin K shots, sometimes daily, usually at no charge. Still she wouldn't heal.

When Doc Chuck said amputation might be the only way to save Kali's life, I knew we had to get a second opinion.

Fortunately Mike's uncle, Dr. Steve Colter, was at a veterinarian conference at the time. We texted photos of Kali's leg to Steve and his colleagues. Within minutes he replied: "Necrosis. Get her to vet hospital ASAP."

We decided to drive the five hours to the veterinary hospital where uncle Steve worked. At that point in our lives, we were fortunate to have the time and money to make the trip, and family there to stay with.

It took Steve's colleagues several surgeries to repair Kali's wound. But still she kept bleeding. Late one night when uncle Steve went to check on Kali, he found her fading fast. And then it came to him — she might have Von Willebrand's, a hereditary bleeding disorder. He gave her a shot of desmopressin that saved her life.

Had we amputated her leg, Kali would have bled to death. Because of uncle Steve and his amazing team at the VCA Veterinary Specialists of Northern Colorado, Kali lived another nine years. NINE YEARS! I am forever grateful.

SECTION TWO:
Ask Your Dear Dog

"Early on I promised my Bernese mountain dog Fleury that she wouldn't be subjected to painful treatments that could only prolong her life — not save it. When Fleury developed Auto-Immune Hemolytic Anemia (AIHA) she received a blood transfusion, but immediately killed off all the new red blood cells. There was no hope, and she hated the experience. When she grew too weak from the anemia, I let her go peacefully as promised."

— *Laura Lee Yates, Fleury's Mom*

What Is Quality of Life?

Taking an honest look at our Dear Dog's quality of life is hard. It isn't a precise science. It's subjective and imperfect and depends on our dog's illness, symptoms and even personality.

Since our pups can't talk, it's up to us as their moms and dads to pay attention to how they're feeling based on their behavior. While there is a physical component to consider — is my Dear Dog hurting? — there is also a psychological component — is my Dear Dog happy?

Just like people, our dogs' quality of life depends on three key areas:

- ♥ Physical Comfort
- ♥ Social Connection
- ♥ Emotional Wellbeing

We'll look at each area one at a time in the next four questions and their accompanying guide sheets. Then we'll bring it all together in a Quality of Life guide sheet.

Remember, our dogs are individuals. Kali, for instance, was very active and loved new adventures and games. Our other dog, Jenna, has always been a quieter doggo who likes routines and cuddles.

Take your dog's unique personality into account when filling out the guide sheets in this section.

Ask for Help

Another person's objective perspective may be invaluable to you for this section — sometimes we are just too close to our furkids to notice gradual changes. You might ask a trusted friend or extended family member to fill out the guide sheets in this section with you. Or ask them to fill out the guide sheets on their own and then meet with you to compare answers and discuss.

Remember our Mantra

This might be a good time to pause, take a breath, place a hand over your heart and repeat our mantra:

"When I listen to my heart, I do good things.
My heart is bigger than my hurt."

Let's get started with Question 3.

SAY MANTRA

Put your hands over your heart and say aloud:

"When I listen to my heart, I do good things."

"My heart is bigger than my hurt."

QUESTION 3

Is my Dear Dog in physical pain?

THE STORY OF GRACIE

Marilyn Colter grew up on a cattle ranch in southeastern Arizona. "I knew when an animal was sick," she says, which is why it came as such a shock when her beloved Border Collie, Gracie, was diagnosed with cancer.

"Gracie was so stoic," Marilyn says. "She never complained about anything."

When they would go hiking, Gracie's herding instinct kicked in. "If I sat down to rest and my friend kept walking, Gracie would run up the trail to my friend as if to say, 'Wait! Wait!' Then she'd run back to me to say, 'Come on! Let's go!'" says Marilyn. "She wanted to keep us together. It was so funny and had me in stitches!"

When their vet, Dr. Susan, diagnosed Gracie with bladder cancer, she explained there was no way to save Gracie. The vet prescribed medication to keep her comfortable.

A few weeks later, Marilyn came home from work. Gracie followed her into the kitchen like usual for her treat. And then Gracie sneezed. "I turned around," Marilyn says, "and the back of my clothing was covered with blood. Blood was just pouring out of her nose."

By the time Marilyn got Gracie into the pickup truck, she was sneezing blood constantly. "I drove as fast as I could," Marilyn says. "I didn't want her to suffer."

When they reached the vet, Gracie had almost bled out and couldn't move. She was crying in pain. Dr. Susan met them outside and euthanized Gracie right there in the backseat of Marilyn's pickup.

"She was the best dog in the world," Marilyn says. "We had been through some hard times together, and she was always there and so sweet. I didn't know what I was going to do without her. She was just the best friend."

WATCH THIS

Marilyn Shares Gracie's Story

WEBSITE:
GoodbyeDearDog.com/videos

"Like people, some dogs are more dramatic than others and will waste no time letting you know if something bothers them. But other dogs are quite stoic and will tolerate discomfort to a much higher degree before protesting — assuming they protest at all."

— *Dr. Jessica Vogelsang, VetStreet.com veterinarian*

Dogs Express Pain Differently

Canines don't express pain the same way we humans do, which is one reason it's sometimes hard to know they're suffering. Another reason is their expression of pain varies, based on their personalities and the amount of pain they're experiencing.

One dog may not show pain the same way another dog does.

Some dogs — like Marilyn's dog Gracie — are stoics. They carry on their usual activities dispassionately until the pain is finally unbearable. Stoic dogs may show only subtle signs of distress, like shifting their eyes away when we look at them or breathing rapidly.

"When Gracie started whining on the car ride to the vet," Marilyn says, "I knew she must really be in pain."

Other dogs — like Laura Lee Yates's dog Fleury — are sensitive. They react dramatically to the slightest bump. Sensitive dogs may show obvious signs of distress, like a sharp cry, growl, snap, bite, or jerking back.

Since our fur kids' expression of pain varies, it's up to us as their parents to notice behavioral changes. Then, with the help of our vet, we can do our best to make them more comfortable.

Pain versus Suffering

For the purposes of this guidebook, let's think about pain and suffering this way:

PAIN is a *physical sensation*.

When we're in acute pain, our heart rate and breathing speed up, and the stress hormone cortisol rises in our bloodstream. The same holds true for our companion animals. But as veterinary consultant Dr. Natalie Stilwell points out, these pain markers are difficult to measure because going to the vet is stressful for most pets.

Unlike human doctors — who can ask their patients questions about their pain — pet doctors cannot. That is why they rely on behavioral changes to evaluate an animal's pain level.

While pain for people or pets is subjective, it definitely signals something is wrong.

SUFFERING is an *emotional sensation*.

When our Dear Dogs are in pain and cannot do what they want, they suffer emotionally. And as much as we want to, we can't explain to them what's happening or assure them it's temporary, if that's the case.

Just like physical pain, we can look for changes in our dogs' personalities and behaviors to understand when they are suffering. There's plenty to keep an eye out for when you know what to look for. Don't worry — we'll cover that next.

> "A major obstacle to effective pain management is the nonverbal nature of animals. Veterinarians and others who work with animals are left to rely on behavioral cues that can be misinterpreted or go unnoticed."
>
> — R. Scott Nolen, *"The Ethics of Pain Management in Animals,"* Journal of American Veterinary Medical Association

Signs of Pain in Our Dear Dogs

"I sure do miss these two beautiful souls," says Jim Howden about his dogs Luna and Mirdog. "I was so blessed to have them in my life, and am grateful to have had them as my best friends. They will always be in my heart."

How can Dog Parents know if our dogs are in pain? I asked my current vet how they measure pain in their dog patients. He showed me the "Canine Acute Pain Scale" tool created by Dr. Peter W. Hellyer and associates at Colorado State University's College of Veterinary Medicine. (I smiled when I heard this — CSU is my alma mater, and uncle Steve taught at the vet school!)

In addition to Dr. Hellyer's scale, I looked at quality of life scales created by veterinarians Dr. Alice Villalobos (Pawspice and Animal Oncology Clinic) and Dr. Dani McVety and Dr. Mary Gardner (Lap of Love Veterinary Hospice) for guidance. I also found the "Making Decisions When Your Companion Animal is Sick" booklet published by the Argus Institute at Colorado State University helpful.

I brought it all together — plus some observations of mine and other Dog Parents — in Guide Sheet #3 on page 36. Here are the most common physical ways our dogs show us something is wrong and they may be in pain:

EMERGENCY!

Get to a **VETERINARIAN IMMEDIATELY** if you see any of these symptoms:

- ☐ Difficulty breathing
- ☐ Uncontrollable vomiting
- ☐ Uncontrollable diarrhea
- ☐ Sudden collapse, fainting, loss of consciousness
- ☐ Panting excessively without stop
- ☐ Pacing while heart racing
- ☐ Profuse bleeding (internally or externally)
- ☐ Continuous whining, crying, yelping or yowling

- ☐ Panting excessively
- ☐ Pacing
- ☐ Whining, whimpering or crying while still
- ☐ Worried look on face (ears flat, eyes wide and/or darting)
- ☐ Growling, snarling, snapping
- ☐ Limping or lameness, unable to get up or move around
- ☐ Falling down, unable to stand
- ☐ Sleeping difficulties
- ☐ Restless (at night or during day)
- ☐ Eating less, or not at all
- ☐ Drinking more or less than usual
- ☐ Flinching when touched
- ☐ Bladder or bowel control problems
- ☐ Lethargic
- ☐ Coughing
- ☐ Vomiting
- ☐ Diarrhea
- ☐ Yelping or crying out when touched or moving

Your initial response to some of these behaviors — such as accidents in the house or snapping at you — may be to reprimand or punish your Dear Dog. If this is unusual behavior, don't scold. More than likely something is wrong physically, and your pup probably feels confused and anxious.

Kali's Signs of Pain in Hindsight

About eight months after Kali's death, I filled out Guide Sheet #3 for her retroactively. I was horrified to see she showed 22 signs of pain. My poor kid! She had seemed so sad, and now I know why.

Some of the signs she had been showing for a year or two. Things like lagging on walks, slipping on the stairs, and pooping while walking without even noticing.

Mike and I chocked a lot of these symptoms up to "old age" at the time. The more extreme signs, like fainting and flinching, happened in the last few months of her life.

My hope is that the following guide sheet helps you interpret your Dear Dog's pain signs better than I did with my Dear Kali.

Before we dig in, though, please read the symptoms in the "Emergency" box on the previous page.

And remember, we're right here with you.

FILL OUT

Physical Signs My Dear Dog Is In Pain on next page

WEBSITE:
GoodbyeDearDog.com/guidesheets

> "If the animal has problems getting up and around — even with medication — or he's pooping in the house even though he's been housebroken for 15 years, maybe it's time to let go. Sometimes it's a blessing for the animal."
>
> — *Dr. Jan Pol, veterinarian on National Geographic's* The Incredible Dr. Pol *Show*

GUIDE SHEET #3

DOG'S NAME: _____ TODAY'S DATE: _____

Physical Signs My Dear Dog Is in Pain

INSTRUCTIONS: Below is a list of physical signs dogs often show when in pain. Check the box next to the signs you're seeing in your dog and then bring this guide sheet to your appointment to discuss with your vet.

BREATHING
- ☐ Difficulty breathing
- ☐ Panting excessively without exertion, unable to stop
- ☐ Coughing or hacking, especially at night

FACE & VOCALIZATIONS
- ☐ Salivating or drooling more than usual
- ☐ Dilated pupils
- ☐ Yawning more than usual
- ☐ Constantly licking self and/or things (furniture, floors, etc.)
- ☐ Worried look on face (flat ears, wide-eyed and/or darting eyes)
- ☐ Licking lips when you approach
- ☐ Growling or snapping when usually doesn't, or when certain body parts touched
- ☐ Yelping, whining, crying or yowling

BODY & MOBILITY
- ☐ Pacing house or yard for hours
- ☐ Sitting, lying or standing "funny" (i.e. legs splayed out awkwardly)
- ☐ Seizures
- ☐ Sudden collapse, fainting, losing consciousness
- ☐ Holding head, limb or tail at odd angle
- ☐ Tucking tail between legs, no longer wagging in greeting
- ☐ Flinching when touched
- ☐ Turning in circles or turning only in one direction
- ☐ Getting stuck in unusual places
- ☐ Limping, stumbling, tripping, falling down
- ☐ Refusing to go on walks, walking slower than usual
- ☐ Difficulty jumping up or climbing stairs
- ☐ Struggling to sit down or get up from a lying position
- ☐ Moving very little or not at all
- ☐ Unable to stand on own, unsteady on feet

NIGHTTIME & SLEEPING
- ☐ Wanting to be outside at night (if usually sleeps indoors)
- ☐ Sleeping more than usual
- ☐ Sleeping in places didn't before (in the closet, i.e.)
- ☐ Restless, pacing the house at night
- ☐ Backward sleep-wake cycle (sleeping during day, up at night)
- ☐ Becoming anxious as darkness approaches ("sundowning")

EATING & DRINKING
- ☐ Eating less than usual, loss of appetite, losing weight
- ☐ Needing to be handfed or enticed to eat
- ☐ Eating more than usual, ravenous appetite
- ☐ Not drinking water at all
- ☐ Drinking noticeably more water than usual
- ☐ Vomiting

GOING POTTY
- ☐ Having accidents in the house, unable to make it outside to go potty
- ☐ Urinating infrequently or more than usual
- ☐ Changing bowel habits, like straining or constipation
- ☐ Diarrhea
- ☐ Pooping while walking, unaware it's happening
- ☐ Pooping or peeing while sleeping
- ☐ Struggling to squat or lift leg to go potty, needing help

OTHER SIGNS I NOTICED & WANT TO ASK VET ABOUT
- ☐ _____
- ☐ _____
- ☐ _____

©2020 Dorothea Deley. www.GoodbyeDearDog.com

KALI'S STORY

One Last Camping Trip

Mike, Kali, Jenna and I loved to camp! We'd hike all day and cuddle up in our sleeping bags at night. When we were nestled together in our little tent, I felt safe and loved.

A few months before our annual spring camping trip, Kali had been tiring easily on neighborhood walks. We had even started leaving her home when we went on local hikes.

A couple days before we left on our trip, her tummy seemed a little swollen to me but not to Mike.

I knew taking Kali camping probably wasn't the best idea. But I didn't want to leave her behind for our annual trip! Plus a quiet voice inside me whispered, "This will be Kali's last camping trip." I went ahead and made a vet appointment for when we returned just to be safe.

As we packed up the tent and cooler, Kali perked up. She had always loved hiking, particularly when there was a creek to cool off in! Watching her scramble into the backseat, Mike and I looked at each other over the car roof and smiled. I felt a pang in my chest, but brushed it aside.

Mike and I agreed that if Kali couldn't hike, one of us would stay behind at the campsite with her. But she was having none of that! Every day she hiked with us. Resting more than usual, sure. But still there, plodding along a few yards behind. Part of me wondered naively if maybe she was fine after all?

Hiking Mile After Mile in Pain

In retrospect, I now know she hiked with us not because she was "fine," but because our Dear Dogs will do just about anything to be near us. They may hide their pain until it's so debilitating they simply cannot go on. Especially stoic dogs like Kali.

And so, desperate not to be separated from her pack, Kali hiked mile after mile. What we didn't know then was her poor heart wasn't working properly.

My heart hurts just thinking about it.

Instead of dwelling on that, though, I choose to remember a sweet moment from that trip. Kali is lying in sand along the creek bank. Red canyon walls rise above her, ablaze with the light of the setting sun. She sniffs the breeze and looks around, taking it all in. She seems peaceful. Happy. Content.

QUESTION

Does my Dear Dog still enjoy favorite activities?

THE STORY OF LOU

Marisa Waddell and her wife, Patti, loved taking their two Chihuahua mixes hiking near their house. Little Lou and Lily loved it too!

A friend and her rambunctious puppy joined them on one of their hikes. As the group started up the first hill, Lou sat down and refused to walk another step.

"We thought he was just being stubborn," Marisa says. "Or maybe acting reticent because of the younger dog. Or maybe he just wanted to be carried, that little rascal!"

Photo by Marisa Waddell

Finally Patti scooped Lou up. "Then he was happy," Marisa says, "because he got to be with us." Later Marisa and Patti found out the real reason Lou didn't want to go up that hill — he had Congestive Heart Failure.

"I wish we had known then that when your dog does something out of character, it might be because he doesn't feel well — not because he's being obstinate," Marisa says. "It may have helped us treat him a little bit more humanely."

After his diagnosis, Marisa and Patti were able to get treatment for Lou, which extended his life for more than a year. That gave them precious time together. Then one morning, Lou woke Marisa and Patti up with his labored breathing. They rushed him to their vet where he was stabilized with oxygen. But Lou needed to get to an emergency vet hospital — and quick.

Their vet called ahead to let the hospital know Lou was on his way. Marisa drove the 20 miles as fast as she could while Patti hugged Lou tight. Sadly, Lou died before they reached the hospital.

Later that day Marisa and Patti held a small ceremony for Lou. They gathered their parents, close friends and godchildren at the family ranch. Everyone shared favorite stories of Lou, laughing and crying together. As the sun set, they buried Lou in his favorite sunny napping spot.

"It was perfect," says Marisa, "A good way to say goodbye."

WATCH THIS

Marisa Shares Lou's Story

WEBSITE: GoodbyeDearDog.com/videos

Activities Your Dog Loves to Do

Like people, dogs have favorite activities they just love to do. And like people, when dogs don't feel well or feel like "themselves," they struggle to do their favorite activities.

What activities bring your Dear Dog joy? What does he just light up to do?

To spark ideas, here are activities many dogs enjoy:

- ♥ walking
- ♥ hiking
- ♥ running
- ♥ swimming
- ♥ cuddling
- ♥ being petted
- ♥ getting tummy tickles
- ♥ eating treats
- ♥ being chased
- ♥ playing keep-a-way
- ♥ playing tug-o-war
- ♥ playing with other dogs
- ♥ playing with toys
- ♥ fetching toys/balls/Frisbees
- ♥ performing tricks
- ♥ looking out a favorite window
- ♥ lying in the sun
- ♥ riding in the car
- ♥ doing other activities unique to your doggie (Kali liked to play hide-and-seek with a toy!)

We'll be referring back to this list for Guide Sheet #4. There's also an easy online tool for you to use to make two pie charts of your Dear Dog's favorite activities — one based on the past when he felt well, and one now. For some of us, seeing a visual image can be helpful.

> "If you have been an earnest observer of your pet's behavior and attitude during his or her lifetime, you will be the best at determining when they no longer seem 'happy.' You'll know when they no longer enjoy food, toys, or the environment around them."
>
> — Dr. Mary Gardner & Dr. Dani McVety, *Lap of Love Veterinary Hospice*

FILL OUT

My Dear Dog's Favorite Activities on page 44

WEBSITE:
GoodbyeDearDog.com/guidesheets

Fave Activities Change Over Time

Your pup's list of favorite activities changes as he ages. That's perfectly normal. The same happens for us, too. Goodness knows I don't go out dancing till one in the morning anymore!

Let me give you an example from Kali's life. As a youngster she loved chasing squirrels — even leaping through screened windows on several occasions to run after them. As she aged, she stopped chasing squirrels and contentedly watched them out the window on what we called Dog TV.

Once we have a list of your dog's favorite activities, we're going to "ask" him (based on his behavior) if he's still able to do . . .

- ♥ most of his favorite activities,
- ♥ some of his favorite activities,
- ♥ adapted versions of his favorite activities, or
- ♥ none of his favorite activities.

A caveat: Some dogs may attempt to do what they love, like chasing a ball, long after they've lost control of other bodily functions. That's why we measured those physical factors separately in Question 3.

"When Paco was home with his routine it was harder to see how poorly he was doing. But at the park I could see he wasn't interested at all in the ducks or the lake or anything he usually enjoyed. He just looked at me like, 'Let's go home.'"

— *Charmin Dahl, Paco's Mom*

In her senior years, Kali spent hours watching the world go by through our front window. She and Jenna loved it so much we called it Dog TV!

Comparing Your Dog's Then & Now Pie Charts

After you fill out Guide Sheet #4 and/or the online pie chart tool, you'll compare your furkid's "Then" and "Now" activity lists.

If your Dear Dog's "Then" and "Now" activity pies are similar to each other and he's not in pain, he's probably still enjoying life. That's great news!

On the other hand, if your best friend's "Then" and "Now" activity pies show an obvious drop in the number of activities he can still enjoy, it may be time to think seriously about his quality of life.

Here are some suggestions going forward:

Fill out a pie chart once a month.

It's so easy to overlook subtle changes that happen slowly over time. Filling out a pie chart once a month can help you keep an eye out for any changes. We'd be happy to send you gentle email reminders once a month — just let us know at the link in the "Get Support" box.

Ask a trusted friend/family member to fill out the pie charts.

Sometimes other people close to your pet see things you may not. Ask someone who loves your dog to fill out the Fave Activities pie charts. Then compare what they see to what you see: Do you both see the same things? Different things? You can also use the pie charts to spark a conversation with family members, especially if someone's been avoiding the topic.

To show you how Guide Sheet #4 and its accompanying online tool work, I filled them out for Kali on the next page.

GET SUPPORT

Request email reminders to fill out Favorite Activity Charts

WEBSITE: GoodbyeDearDog.com/support

Kali's Favorite Activities: Then & Now

In the last couple years of her life, Kali had mellowed quite a bit. She still enjoyed her favorite activities — in modified forms. Her favorite activities at age 13 looked like this:

- ♥ Going on walks
- ♥ Fetching toys
- ♥ Playing hide-n-seek with toy
- ♥ Cuddling on the couch
- ♥ Riding in the car
- ♥ Swimming (in pools, lakes, creeks, ocean)
- ♥ Eating red meat
- ♥ Playing peek-a-boo under a shirt
- ♥ Waking me up every morning by scratching my side of bed
- ♥ Watching Dog TV with her sister Jenna

THEN:
Age 13, June 2012
When Kali Felt Good

Now that's a pretty well-rounded life! Even for a granny!

Kali enjoyed all kinds of activities and did them all frequently, even if she couldn't walk as fast or fetch as many balls as she used to.

Without a doubt she was happiest when she could do her favorite activities — even modified versions of them.

Two years later when she didn't feel so well, Kali could only do 2 of her 10 fave activities:

- ♥ Eating red meat
- ♥ Riding in car

NOW:
Age 15, June 2015
When Kali Felt Bad

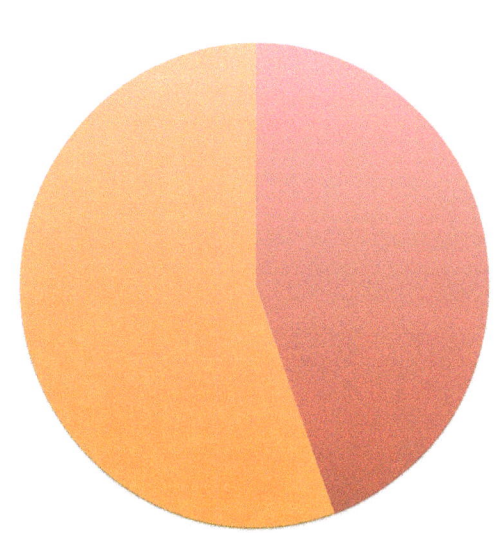

Kali's life had shrunk from 10 activities to 2: eating meat and riding in the car. The truth is even those activities weren't all that joyful for her anymore.

Often she had to eat lying down because she was unsteady on her feet. Several times I even had to hand feed her because the heart meds made her nauseous.

Riding in the car no longer meant going on another great adventure. Now it meant another trip to the vet. A couple times Kali even fainted when we lifted her out of the car.

I couldn't argue with the heartbreaking pie chart: Kali was hurting and could no longer do most of the things that brought her so much joy.

That's no life for my baby.

....

Key to Kali's Fave Activities

- 🟦 going on walks
- 🟥 eating meat
- 🟩 waking me up
- 🟪 peekaboo under shirt
- 🟦 watching Dog TV out window
- 🟧 riding in the car
- 🟦 fetching toys
- 🟪 swimming
- 🟨 cuddling on couch
- 🟪 playing hide-n-seek w/toy

FILL OUT

My Dear Dog's Favorite Activities on next page

WEBSITE:
GoodbyeDearDog.com/ guidesheets

SECTION TWO: ASK YOUR DEAR DOG

GUIDE SHEET #4

DOG'S NAME: _____   TODAY'S DATE: _____

My Dear Dog's Favorite Activities

STEP 1 INSTRUCTIONS: Make a list of your Dear Dog's top 6 – 10 favorite activities from when he was healthier — when he felt more like "himself" or at the peak of his life. (See page 39 for ideas.) On a scale of 1 to 5, rate the degree to which he was interested in and able to enjoy each activity in the "THEN" column. Do the same in the "NOW" column.

Favorite Activities	To What Degree Able to Engage In and Enjoy This Favorite Activity? 1 = Not at all interested or able 3 = Somewhat interested and/or able 5 = Enthusiastically interested and able	
	THEN	**NOW**
1.		
2.		
3.		
4.		
5.		
6.		
7.		
8.		
9.		
10.		

FILL OUT

Favorite Activities Pie Charts online

WEBSITE:
GoodbyeDearDog.com/piecharts

©2020 Dorothea Deley. www.GoodbyeDearDog.com

GUIDE SHEET #4 (continued)

STEP 2 INSTRUCTIONS: Would you like a visual representation of your Dear Dog's changing activities? Go to **GoodbyeDearDog.com/piecharts** and enter the info from page 44 to automatically generate your dog's "Then" and "Now" Favorite Activities Pie Charts. Print them out (or save a screenshot) and attach them below.

Favorite Activities Pie Charts

STEP 3 INSTRUCTIONS: Based on the chart on page 44 and/or the pie charts above, answer the following questions.

1. **My dog's "Then" and "Now" charts are:** *(check one)*
   - ☐ radically different
   - ☐ somewhat different
   - ☐ pretty similar

2. **My dog used to be able to do** *(insert number)* _____ **favorite activities.**

   Now he can do *(insert number)* _____ **of those favorite activities.**

3. **My Dear Dog seems:** *(check one)*
   - ☐ okay not being able to do his favorite activities
   - ☐ sad not being able to do his favorite activities

4. **When I look at these two "Then" and "Now" charts for my Dear Dog, I feel:**

   _____

   _____

   _____

   _____

©2020 Dorothea Deley. www.GoodbyeDearDog.com

KALI'S STORY

The Day Kali Retired from Fetch

Australian cattle dogs were bred to herd cows, but they'll settle for chasing anything you can throw or kick! Kali lived for playing fetch. FETCH-FETCH-FETCH!

Sometimes Kali's obsession got to be a little embarrassing, like the time we had friends over for dinner. While we chatted over eggplant Parmesan, Kali — unbeknownst to us — kept putting slobbery balls in our friend Molly's lap beneath the table! When Molly stood up toys fell everywhere. Hilarious.

Kali loved diving into ocean waves after a toy — particularly her rubber dumbbell. When we moved inland, she loved jumping into my parents' pool after the dumbbell. A few months before we understood how compromised her heart had become, I took her over to my parents for a swim.

She yipped excitedly when I pulled out her toy, and ran over to the side of the pool. I tossed the dumbbell in the water and Kali leapt after it. She grabbed for the toy, slowly swam back, and struggled to get out of the pool. And then ... she dropped the toy in the grass and walked away.

Was she still interested in doing her favorite activity? Yes, definitely. But was she able to do it? No.

WATCH THIS

Kali Dives for Toy

WEBSITE:
GoodbyeDearDog.com/videos

My Fuzzy Alarm Clock

Some changes in Kali's favorite activities were obvious — like that day at the pool when she walked away from fetch. Other changes were so subtle I didn't notice them at first. Here's one example.

Later in life one of Kali's favorite activities (mine, too!) was waking me up every morning by scratching on my side of the bed. Then I'd reach down and give her a hug and a kiss. She especially loved it if I blew my morning breath in her face, which always made me laugh. What a fun way to wake up! (No wonder we love our dogs, right?!)

One morning I realized my "Kali Alarm" hadn't gone off. Confused, I looked around for Kali — there she was on her bed, still sleeping. Then I tried to remember the last time she had woken me up... A few weeks ago? A couple months ago? Had it really been that long?!?

It had. I just hadn't noticed.

QUESTION

Is my Dear Dog withdrawing socially?

THE STORY OF BAILEY

John Thompson's Labrador Weimaraner mix Bailey loved to play catch. "You couldn't throw a tennis ball enough times or far enough for her!" he says. "She was a joyful soul with a ball in her mouth."

Bailey was loyal, too. "She was always by my side," John says, "often with her head in my lap."

As Bailey aged, she slowed down. At first John noticed little changes, like her not being to able hop out of the car or not wanting to chase the ball as often.

"When you start seeing those behavioral changes," he says, "they're coming on so slowly you don't really realize that your pet's in a lot of pain."

It wasn't until Bailey stopped hanging out with the family and spent most of her time lying in the back hallway that John understood how much pain she was in.

"She just wasn't herself. No interest in companionship, which was really different."

After several false starts, John finally made the euthanasia call to the vet. When the vet came to their house, John took her to the back hallway and sat on the floor next to Bailey. He gently laid her head in his lap and petted her as the doctor gave her the injections.

"Bailey relaxed for the first time in a year-and-a-half," John says. "It hadn't been so obvious to me how much pain she'd been in. How much she was holding it in her body until there was just that relaxation, that letting go."

It hurt to lose his constant companion of 15 years. It was also a relief because now she was at peace and not in pain anymore.

"I miss her head in my lap and just rubbing her ears," John says. "Bailey had the softest ears. I miss those gentle moments of comradeship and love."

WATCH THIS

John Shares Bailey's Story

WEBSITE:
GoodbyeDearDog.com/ videos

SECTION TWO: ASK YOUR DEAR DOG   47

Withdrawing from the Pack

Canines are pack animals. By their very nature they're social. When you adopt your Dear Dog and bring her home, your family becomes her pack and you her substitute parent.

> "When a healthy human-animal bond is no longer possible, the caregiver must be made aware that the end is near."
>
> — *Dr. Alice Villalobos, Pawspice Founder & Veterinarian Oncologist*

Many of our Dear Dogs will do just about anything to be with their pack, won't they? Like Kali trudging along on her last camping trip even though she felt poorly.

That's why it's important to take note when you see changes in how your Dear Dog connects with you and others. Now if she's always been aloof or a loner, that's one thing. But if this is new behavior, it means something.

For instance, if your cuddle-bunny no longer seeks your affection, you'll know she's not feeling well.

If she's usually a social butterfly, greeting friends with curious sniffs and tail wags, but now she's hiding out in the laundry room, you'll know she's not feeling well.

Or if she's no longer barking at the plumber like she used to, protecting her territory, you'll know she's not feeling well.

On the flip-side, if your gal is usually independent and suddenly acts needy and clingy, you'll know she's not feeling well.

Each Dog is Different

Like everything else in this guidebook, Question #5 really depends on your Dear Dog. The point is to look for changes that might otherwise go unnoticed.

Sometimes a social behavioral change is the first sign something is wrong. Other times it's the last sign, the one that alerts you she's ready to go.

Overlooking social withdrawal — like John thinks he did with Bailey — may cause both of you undue suffering. Physical suffering for your dog; emotional suffering for you.

Don't worry if you're not sure what changes to look out for. Guide Sheet #5 on the next page will help you.

Gustavo Brett's dogs, Sidney (left) and Rosie, were best buds before Sidney passed. They did everything together, and especially loved cuddling!

"Our little Pomeranian, Missy, loved cuddling on my lap and sleeping next to my husband. When she developed dementia, she hid in our closet all day and only came out to eat. It was really sad to see our affectionate little love bug like that. Still breaks my heart all these years later."

— *Margie Rensky, Missy's Mom*

FILL OUT

Signs My Dear Dog Is Withdrawing on next page

WEBSITE:
GoodbyeDearDog.com/guidesheets

SECTION TWO: ASK YOUR DEAR DOG 49

GUIDE SHEET #5

DOG'S NAME: _____ TODAY'S DATE: _____

Signs My Dear Dog Is Withdrawing Socially

INSTRUCTIONS: Check the boxes next to any social changes *that are NEW* for your dog. (For instance, if she's *always* been disinterested in other dogs there's no need to mark that behavior down below.) Even if your dog appears healthy physically, these signs could point to an undiagnosed health issue or cognitive decline. If you check any boxes, bring this guide sheet to your next appointment to discuss with your vet.

SOCIAL INTERACTION WITH YOU
- ☐ Greeting you with a happy tail wag less often than usual, or not at all
- ☐ Refusing to hang out with rest of family (i.e. in living room while you watch TV, beneath the table while you eat dinner)
- ☐ Withdrawing from other pets in your household if used to play/sleep/cuddle with them
- ☐ Spending most of the time hiding — under the bed, in a closet, behind the couch, or another location
- ☐ Averting gaze when looked at
- ☐ Sleeping away from family (when usually would sleep near you)
- ☐ Needing to be in constant contact with you; acting needy and clingy when used to be more independent
- ☐ Suffering from severe separation anxiety when left alone

INTERACTING WITH OTHERS
- ☐ Showing no interest in people you pass on walks
- ☐ Showing no interest in dogs you pass on walks
- ☐ Showing no interest in visitors who come to the door or into your home

REACTION TO TOUCH
- ☐ Avoiding being petted or cuddled, sometimes even moving away

OTHER SOCIAL CHANGES I HAVE NOTICED
- ☐ _____
- ☐ _____
- ☐ _____

©2020 Dorothea Deley. www.GoodbyeDearDog.com

KALI'S STORY

From Lap Dog to Loner Dog

Mike and I adopted Kali from an animal shelter. Not only had her original family surrendered her, she had been adopted and returned to the shelter twice before we found her!

That may explain why Kali hated to be separated from us. She'd bark her little head off when we left the house without her. She'd try to sit on my lap in the car instead of in the backseat — and at 40 pounds she wasn't exactly a lap dog!

Usually when we went on trips without her, friends and relatives babysat for us. In all the years we had her, we only boarded her once. Here's why:

A few hours after we left her at the pet hotel, we got a call from the kennel manager.

"We wanted to let you know," she said, "that Kali jumped out of her dog run, which has a six-foot fence around it. And then she somehow got over our eight-foot perimeter fence. No dog has ever jumped that fence before!"

Mike and I held our breath and waited for the rest of the story.

"She took off running down the road but we were able to call her back. She's safe now."

Mike and I sighed in relief. We decided to pick Kali up a day early, and I'm so thankful we did. When we arrived, we found her curled up in a ball on the concrete floor of her kennel, looking despondent. I'm sure she thought we had returned her too.

"Oh Baby Bups!" I hugged her and cried. "We would never leave you."

Slowly Kali Pulls Away

When we drove to southern Utah for Kali's final camping trip, she didn't try to sit on my lap once.

Two months later, Kali started sleeping out in the hallway instead of in our bedroom.

And then she stopped wagging her tail when we returned home.

And finally, whenever I hugged her she'd get up and move away instead of putting her paw on my shoulder and nuzzling me like she used to.

There was no denying it now. Our Kali was hurting.

QUESTION

Has my Dear Dog's personality or emotional state changed?

THE STORY OF MITCH

Construction worker Tony Perrotti rescued his dog, Mitch, during a low point in both their lives.

"I had just gone through a painful divorce," Tony says, "and coming home to an empty house every day was really depressing."

When Tony went to the animal shelter and saw Mitch, he thought, "What a big lug of a dog. Kinda like me!" Then he found out 1-year-old Mitch was scheduled to be put down that very afternoon — for aggression.

"I figured, what the hell. I got nothing to lose and he's got everything to gain. So I took him home."

Mitch and Tony became fast friends. "It was tough at first, but he mellowed out," Tony says. "He was my buddy, my boy." For the next 11 years Mitch and Tony weathered the ups and downs of life — new relationships, changing jobs, and deaths of loved ones.

"He was there for all of it," Tony says, "He even fell in love with my fiancé right along with me. She won him over with dog biscuits!"

Eventually Mitch's old joints ached with arthritis. He stopped chasing his ball. He couldn't manage the steps to the backyard on his own anymore. And then, he started acting aggressive — something he hadn't done since Tony first adopted him.

Adobe Stock Image

"He'd be fine with me. But whenever someone else tried to pet him, he'd growl and snap." Tony didn't understand that Mitch was acting out because he was in pain, so he'd yell at him, "Hey, cut it out!"

Tony's fiancé helped him see the truth about Mitch's condition and make the decision to euthanize. "He was 12 years old," Tony says, "Even pain medication didn't help and he just hurt all over. I didn't want him to be sad and in pain anymore."

While losing Mitch was heartbreaking, Tony says, "He taught me a lot about second chances, about tolerance and patience. I will always love him."

Every Dog's Personality Is Unique

Every dog has his or her own unique personality. As Dog Parents, we know that firsthand, don't we?!

Some dogs are playful, always clowning around. Others are mellow, happy to hang out on a lap. You know your Dear Dog's personality best.

Photo by Theo Waddell

Just like people, our dogs can experience depression or anxiety. Sometimes these feelings might be because of a change at home or in the family.

For example, have you recently moved? Has a child left for college? Has another pet died?

Other times, like with Tony's dog Mitch, emotional and personality changes mean something is physically wrong. There might be an underlying health problem.

Since our furkids can't speak to us, we need to pay close attention to cues they may be giving about how they are feeling.

Dogs Hate Feeling Vulnerable

In her book *Animals in Translation*, animal behavioral expert Temple Grandin explains that canines are predator animals. When they're physically vulnerable — like Mitch, who could no longer get around on his own — they naturally become stressed and anxious.

Why? Because they cannot do their most important jobs:

- ♥ protect themselves,
- ♥ defend their territory, and
- ♥ alert and defend their pack.

When some dogs are anxious, they may snap or growl. Other dogs might hide or withdraw.

When our dogs act out or display unusual-for-them behavior, our first reaction might be to reprimand them or ignore them.

Instead we need to think about the emotional toll physical vulnerability takes on our Dear Dogs. It's as stressful for them as it is for humans who are physically compromised.

So now we have a dog who is suffering physical pain as well as emotional stress. The worst part is we as dog owners may not understand what's really going on.

READ MORE

Temple Grandin's Book *Animals in Translation*

WEBSITE: GoodbyeDearDog.com/resources

When Cognitive Changes Affect Personality

As we were wrapping up this book, our sweet 17-year-old dog, Jenna, had a stroke. Overnight she went from herself to a dog we didn't recognize with odd new behaviors.

She'd pace the house in the same repetitive pattern, from her bed to the living room to my office to her doggie door and outside in a loop around the backyard and then back inside. Then she'd repeat the entire loop. Over and over. For hours. It was upsetting to watch. It was tiring for her.

She forgot how to eat and drink. I had to hand feed Jenna her meals. And when she drank, water dribbled out of her mouth.

> "Sometimes, when dogs with advanced dementia still have fairly healthy bodies, we can't see [their suffering]."
>
> — Eileen Anderson, Cricket's Mom, *Dog Dementia Help & Support Website*

Jenna had just been hiking the month before, and this change was upsetting. "I don't like it," Mike said. "It's part of the end. She's starting to look sad."

Over the next few months she seemed to get a bit better. She regained much of her functionality. Sometimes she even had a surge of energy on our walks — running so fast I couldn't keep up!

But our vet explained Jenna had suffered neurological damage and now had Canine Cognitive Dysfunction (CCD or doggie dementia). He said we should expect a progressive decline.

And that's exactly what happened. She was confused and forgetful. Sometimes she'd wander off in the middle of eating and leave her bowl full of food. She had four accidents in the house at night. She'd wander in circles and sometimes her hind legs would slide out from under her. Sometimes she even snapped at us — something she had never done before.

Eventually Jenna started getting stuck in the oddest places — inside a kitchen stool, behind the couch tangled in lamp cords, beneath my nightstand. She started pacing again, this time at night, waking us up when she got stuck someplace and needed help. The only time she seemed happy was during her daily walks.

I'm sharing Jenna's story here because making the euthanasia decision for a cognitively ill dog feels different than for a dog that is physically ill. Jenna's body seemed to work fine, whereas Kali's obviously didn't. Jenna didn't seem to be in pain, while Kali clearly was. But Jenna wasn't herself anymore.

If your furbaby is struggling with CCD too, I highly recommend Eileen Anderson's helpful dog dementia website (see link in the "Read More" box).

READ MORE

Doggie Dementia Support

WEBSITE:
GoodbyeDearDog.com/resources

Help Your Dog by Noticing Personality Changes

When our dogs experience emotional stress and exhibit signs of anxiety or depression, it is our responsibility to help them feel better. We do that by digging deeper:

- ♥ **Are they bored and not getting enough stimulation?** — Then we need to schedule play and/or walk time with them.
- ♥ **Are they in physical pain?** — Then we need to work with a vet to address the underlying issue.

> "Most pets are tremendously easy to please, so when it no longer becomes possible to raise a purr or a tail-wag, you should be considering what kind of quality of life your pet is experiencing."
>
> — *Drs. Mary Gardner & Dani McVety, Lap of Love Veterinary Hospice*

It's so important to consider physical pain as a cause for any changes you notice in your furbaby's emotional state. A visit to your vet can help you find out if that's the case, and if so, how to help your Dear Dog feel more comfortable physically so she can feel better emotionally too.

Changes May Be Gradual or Abrupt

When changes are abrupt or radical, we're more likely to notice them. But if our dog's changes are gradual or subtle, we may adapt to the changes as they happen and not even notice them. That's why we're going to ask you to fill out Guide Sheet #6, even if you think your dog's personality hasn't changed.

Our starting point will be your pup's "normal" emotional state and personality — when she acted like herself. That will be your dog's baseline for you to compare any new or unusual changes to.

Of course it's natural for our Dear Dogs' personalities to change over time (just like us, right?!). So be sure to compare a time frame of no more than two years.

Let's get started.

FILL OUT

Emotional & Personality Changes on next page

WEBSITE: GoodbyeDearDog.com/guidesheets

SECTION TWO: ASK YOUR DEAR DOG   55

GUIDE SHEET #6

DOG'S NAME: _____ TODAY'S DATE: _____

Noticing Emotional & Personality Changes in My Dear Dog

STEP 1 INSTRUCTIONS: Think back to when your Dear Dog acted like herself — no more than two years ago. Write the approximate date (month/year) below. That'll be your dog's "baseline." Look at the list of personality traits in the dog illustration. Circle all the ones that match what your Dear Dog's personality and emotional state were like back then.

THEN

Approximate Month & Year: _____

Active
Adventurous
Affectionate Afraid
Aggressive Aloof
Anxious Apathetic
Boisterous Bored
Calm Clumsy Confident
Cuddly Curious Dependent
Depressed Distrustful Domineering Eager-to-Please
Energetic Excitable Fearful Friendly Frustrated Full-of-Character
Gentle Good-natured Goofball Happy Independent Intelligent
Jealous Kid-friendly Lapdog Lazy Lively Loving Loyal Needy
Neurotic Obedient Obstinate OCD Outgoing Playful Possessive
Protective Quiet Relaxed Reserved Self-sufficient Sensitive
Shy Simple Social Strong-willed Stubborn Submissive
Territorial Timid Tolerant Trainable Trickster Trusting
Unaffectionate Uneasy Worried
Other _____

©2020 Dorothea Deley. www.GoodbyeDearDog.com

GUIDE SHEET #6 (continued)

STEP 2 INSTRUCTIONS: Write in today's date below. Circle the traits your Dear Dog exhibits now in the dog below.

STEP 3 INSTRUCTIONS: Look at the "Then" and "Now" dogs and answer the following questions.

1. What do you notice? _____
   _____
   _____

NOW
Today's Date: _____

Active
Adventurous
Affectionate Afraid
Aggressive Aloof Anxious
Apathetic Boisterous Bored
Calm Clumsy Confident
Cuddly Curious
Dependent Depressed
Distrustful Domineering Eager-to-Please Energetic
Excitable Fearful Friendly Frustrated Full-of-Character Gentle
Good-natured Goofball Happy Independent Intelligent Jealous
Kid-friendly Lapdog Lazy Lively Loving Loyal Needy Neurotic
Obedient Obstinate OCD Outgoing Playful Possessive
Protective Quiet Relaxed Reserved Self-sufficient Sensitive
Shy Simple Social Strong-willed Stubborn Submissive
Territorial Timid Tolerant Trainable Trickster Trusting
Unaffectionate Uneasy Worried
Other _____

2. Are there major changes in your Dear Dog's personality and emotional state? If so, what in particular? _____
   _____
   _____

3. Which changes do you want to mention to your vet? _____
   _____
   _____

©2020 Dorothea Deley. www.GoodbyeDearDog.com

KALI'S STORY

From Curious and Playful to Worried and Reserved

When Kali was about 8 years old, we lived at the end of a rural road in western Colorado. One morning I let her outside like usual. Instead of returning to the kitchen to make tea, though, I paused at the door and watched her.

Kali ran across our field toward the dirt road, where a teenaged girl waited for the school bus. When the girl saw my dog, she yelled out, "KALI!"

They met at the fence, Kali standing on her hind legs happily wagging her tail while the girl hugged and petted her. Clearly this greeting of theirs was a morning ritual.

Watching them, I realized Kali had a whole life of her own that I didn't even know about. I mean, look at that — she had her own friends!

Photo by Dorothea Deley

Kali also loved adventures, especially car trips. Every time the suitcases or backpacks came out, she'd get so excited. While we loaded the car she'd slip out of the house and hop into the driver's seat. She'd sit there impatiently, whining as if to say, "Hurry up! Let's get this show on the road!"

In the last few months of Kali's life, I went out of town twice and Mike and I took a trip together once. That meant suitcases came out three times total. Not once did Kali act excited or even remotely interested.

And when some of Kali's favorite people came for a visit, she didn't even greet them.

Clearly she didn't feel like her self.

Kali's Changing Personality

Independent and curious, adventurous and playful were such big traits of Kali's personality. When they started to wane, Mike and I definitely noticed. "Just getting older," we thought. While that's true, she was also in the early stages of heart failure.

When I filled out Guide Sheet #6 for Kali retroactively, I could see the stark difference. Here are her results:

When Kali Felt Like Herself
APRIL 2014

Active
Adventurous
Affectionate
Confident
Curious
Energetic
Excitable
Eager-to-Please
Friendly
Full-of-Character
Independent
Intelligent
Kid-friendly
Loyal
Neurotic
Obedient
OCD
Outgoing
Playful
Sensitive
Strong-willed
Trainable

When Kali Felt Unwell
JUNE 2015

Apathetic
Dependent
Depressed
Distrustful
Quiet
Reserved
Unaffectionate
Uneasy
Worried

QUESTION

7 *How is my Dear Dog's quality of life?*

THE STORY OF KOA

Singer-songwriter Craig Nuttycombe adopted Koa when he was 8 years old. Part Bernese mountain dog, Koa had long hair with a strip on his back that stood up like a punk-rock Mohawk!

One summer Craig asked the groomer to leave Koa's "Mohawk" long just for fun. "He looked so cool!" Craig says. A few days later, Craig and Koa were walking in the park when a guy called out to his friend, "Hey Louie! Look! The dog has a haircut just like yours!" Everybody cracked up — including Craig!

"Koa brought a lot of good cheer and love wherever he went," he says. "That's why I call him my 'Buddha Dog.'"

Just two years into their relationship, Koa developed bladder cancer. Soon after Craig knew it was time to say goodbye.

"Koa never complained or showed his pain," Craig says, "but I could tell he was hurting from the way he moved and spent time laying in one place."

Photo by Craig Nuttycombe

LISTEN UP

Craig's Song
"Go Outside"

WEBSITE:
GoodbyeDearDog.com/
audios

Craig wanted to let Koa go while he still had his pride and dignity — before his quality of life declined further. He also wanted to say goodbye at home instead of in a vet's office.

When the day came, Craig laid on the floor with Koa. "I told him I loved him and that he is a good dog. He gave me one last lick on my cheek."

While saying goodbye to Koa was painful, it was also kind and loving.

"He was the fourth dog of my so-called adult life," Craig says. "Even though we only had two years together, he was the hardest one to let go. Koa has a very special place in my heart and life!"

You can hear one of Craig's dog-inspired songs at the link in the "Listen Up" box.

SAYING GOODBYE TO YOUR DEAR DOG

Understanding Quality of Life

Veterinarians use the phrase "quality of life" often. But what does it really mean?

Quality of life encompasses our dog's physical, emotional and social well being — everything we've explored in the first six questions.

How do we know when our Dear Dog's quality of life is compromised? Many of us struggle with this question. Certainly all the Dog Parents we interviewed did.

At the very minimum, a dog should be able to handle normal bodily functions on her own (see the list below). She should be free from debilitating pain, too.

Minimum Quality of Life Checklist

At a minimum, dogs — even sick ones — should be able to:

- ♥ eat and drink on their own
- ♥ sleep comfortably
- ♥ breathe normally
- ♥ show interest in what's going on around them
- ♥ exercise mildly
- ♥ control their bowels and bladder (unless affected by disease)
- ♥ live free of severe pain

You might be thinking, "Oh good! My Dear Dog can do all of that." Keep in mind this is the *minimum* quality of life. At some point, we have to ask ourselves: Is this the life I want for my beloved pet?

> "Owners experiencing the decline or terminal illness of a pet for the first time will generally wait until the very end to make that difficult decision. They are fearful of doing it too soon and giving up without a good fight. Afterwards, however, most of these owners regret waiting too long. They ... feel guilty for putting their pet through those numerous trips to the vet or uncomfortable medical procedures that did not improve their pet's quality of life."
>
> — *Drs. Mary Gardner & Dani McVety, Lap of Love Veterinary Hospice*

READ MORE

Temple Grandin's Op-Ed "Consider the Animal"

WEBSITE:
GoodbyeDearDog.com/
resources

Treatments Can Affect Quality of Life

Considering quality of life can also help us make decisions about what kinds of treatment to choose for our dogs.

Temple Grandin is a professor of animal science at Colorado State University and author of *Animals Make Us Human: Creating the Best Life for Animals*. (You may have seen the movie made about her life starring Claire Danes!)

In her 10/1/14 *The New York Times* op-ed, Temple suggests we make an important distinction when considering treatment for our Dear Dogs:

> *"There is also an important difference between people and pets. A person understands why they are undergoing a painful or stressful procedure in order to obtain a benefit. A pet does not understand this. That distinction matters when you are considering how a treatment will affect quality of life. One must ask, 'Will this procedure improve my pet's quality of life?'"*

You can read Temple Grandin's "Consider the Animal, Not Just the Cost" op-ed at the link in the "Read More" box.

READ MORE

Tracking Good/
Bad Days

WEBSITE:
GoodbyeDearDog.com/
resources

Happy & Healthy or Sad & Suffering?

Guide Sheet #7 will help you decide if your kiddo is happy and healthy or sad and suffering.

We're going to bring together all the other guide sheets you've filled out up until this point to create a big picture of your Dear Dog's quality of life.

Do your best to be honest!

Don't be surprised if you find yourself going through moments of denial about your Dear Dog's quality of life. We all do.

Think back to John's difficulty accepting that his old gal Bailey was in pain and unhappy. Or Marisa's assumption that her little guy Lou was just being obstinate on their hike.

Or my refusal to see Kali's slowing down wasn't just a normal part of aging but an actual illness.

ALL of us experience denial at some point with our beloved dogs.

How could we not?

If you find yourself "forgetting" about a change in your Dear Dog's behavior, or noticing it and then justifying it with a:

- ♥ "She's just extra tired today,"
- ♥ "It's a natural part of aging," or
- ♥ "I don't know what's gotten in to him today..."

Then you may be experiencing denial. That's why I want you to ask a family member or close friend who knows your pooch to fill out a copy of the guide sheet too. Then the two of you can sit down together and compare results.

You might also consider tracking good and bad days for your Dear Dog. See our website for a discussion of the pros and cons of tracking, as well as a tool to help you, here: GoodbyeDearDog.com/resources

While the "quality of life" question can be daunting, don't worry! We're right here with you. Let's start by having you fill out Guide Sheet #7 on the next page.

READ MORE

Steven Rowley's book *Lily & the Octopus*

WEBSITE: GoodbyeDearDog.com/resources

LILY & THE OCTOPUS

Steven Rowley's beautiful novel is a fictionalized retelling of his experience with his 12-year-old Dachshund Lily. They share one final adventure together as he comes to terms with Lily's impending death.

Lily and the Octopus explores the depths of a Dog Parent's love, heartbreaking denial, and eventual acceptance of his Dear Dog's illness. Yes you'll cry. But you'll feel less alone in your journey with your own dog.

Find the book at your library or purchase at the link in the "Read More" box.

FILL OUT

Evaluating Quality of Life on page 64

WEBSITE: GoodbyeDearDog.com/guidesheets

GUIDE SHEET #7

DOG'S NAME: _____ TODAY'S DATE: _____

Evaluating My Dear Dog's Quality of Life

PART 1 INSTRUCTIONS: Think about how your dog has behaved over the past week. Read the options in the chart below and mark the one(s) that fit your dog for most of those days (4 or more days out of the last 7). If you're not sure, look back at Guide Sheets #3, #4, #5 and #6. Then add up the scores for each category for a total score.

PHYSICAL COMFORT

☐	Struggles to breathe **(EMERGENCY! Go to Vet)**	Breathes normally and without strain	☐
☐	Shows signs of pain, such as: • panting heavily without exertion • pacing • whining • hiding or avoiding interaction • growling, snarling, snapping or flinching when touched • limping • restless at night; pacing or other unusual nighttime behavior	Lives pain-free, or with minor pain managed with medication or supplements and/or other therapies	☐
☐	Struggles to get up, and sometimes needs help; moves with difficulty and may fall down; unable to squat or lift leg to go potty; difficulty standing; difficulty lying down	Gets up and moves around on own without any problem	☐
☐	Eats too little/not at all, has to be hand fed or enticed to eat, or inexplicably ravenous all the time; drinks too much or too little water; eating inappropriate materials (poop, garbage) when usually wouldn't	Eats and drinks normally	☐
☐	Constipated, diarrhea, straining or other changes in bowel habits; urinates often or not at all; incontinent — accidents in the house or on walks without stopping	Goes potty on own just fine	☐

-_____ # of boxes checked this column   # of boxes checked this column +_____

Add the number of boxes checked in the left column to the number in the right column.

Example: (-4) + (+1) = -3   TOTAL PHYSICAL COMFORT SCORE: _____

©2020 Dorothea Deley. www.GoodbyeDearDog.com

64   SAYING GOODBYE TO YOUR DEAR DOG

GUIDE SHEET #7 (continued)

EMOTIONAL WELLBEING

☐	Unable to enjoy favorite activities	Enjoys favorite activities (modified if needed)	☐
☐	Depressed, lethargic, apathetic or disengaged	Playful, engaged, joyful	☐
☐	Stressed, anxious, worried	Calm and relaxed (or whatever your dog's usual "resting" state looks like)	☐
☐	Confused or disoriented, unaware of surroundings; staring at wall; turning in slow circles or always to one direction; getting stuck in unusual places (behind furniture, in corners)	Lucid, aware of and engaged with surroundings; walks in a straight line and able to turn both left and right; able to navigate around furniture and rooms without assistance	☐
☐	Unable to (or not interested in) defending territory/family in usual ways	Defends territory and family in usual ways	☐
-_____	# boxes checked this column	# of boxes checked this column +_____	

Add the number of boxes checked in the left column to the number in the right column.

Example: (-4) + (+1) = -3   TOTAL EMOTIONAL WELLBEING SCORE: _____

SOCIAL CONNECTION

☐	Withdraws from family; avoids interacting; hides; sleeps in unusual places	Wants to hang out with rest of family; enjoys interacting or just being near you, like while you watch TV	☐
☐	Snarls/growls/nips at or avoids/ignores other pets when didn't before	Behaves like usual toward other pets, playing with, nuzzling, sniffing, or at least acknowledging them	☐
☐	Apathetic toward visitors and unfamiliar dogs, even ones entering her "territory" (home and yard)	Greets visitors and unfamiliar dogs with curiosity or defensiveness (whichever is the norm for your dog)	☐
☐	Avoids affection, no longer enjoys affection such as petting and cuddling — moves away instead	Shows affection like usual (whatever that is for your Dear Dog); enjoys petting and cuddling	☐
☐	Ignores you when you come home or greets you with a limp unwagging tail	Greets you with a tail-wag when you return home, happy to see you	☐
-_____	# of boxes checked this column	# of boxes checked this column +_____	

Add the number of boxes checked in the left column to the number in the right column.

Example: (-4) + (+1) = -3   TOTAL SOCIAL CONNECTION SCORE: _____

©2020 Dorothea Deley. www.GoodbyeDearDog.com

GUIDE SHEET #7 (continued)

PART 2a INSTRUCTIONS: Look at the total scores for each of the charts on page 64 and 65. Circle or mark those scores on the corresponding continuums below.

PHYSICAL COMFORT

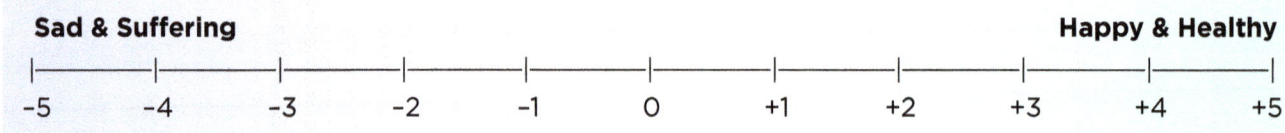

EMOTIONAL WELLBEING

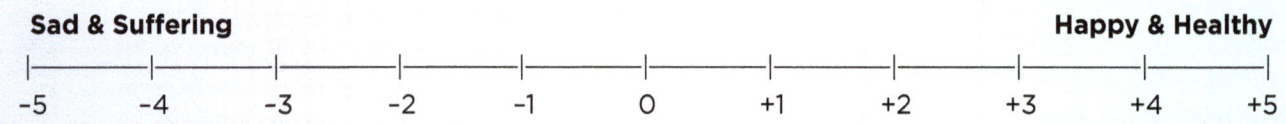

SOCIAL CONNECTION

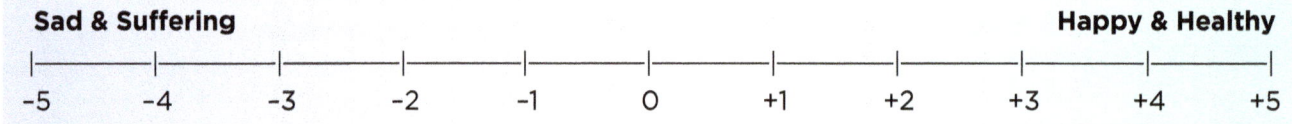

PART 2b INSTRUCTIONS: Now add all three scores together — physical, emotional and social — and divide by 3 to arrive at your Dear Dog's quality of life score. (See page 69 for Kali's example.) Mark that number on the continuum below.

QUALITY OF LIFE

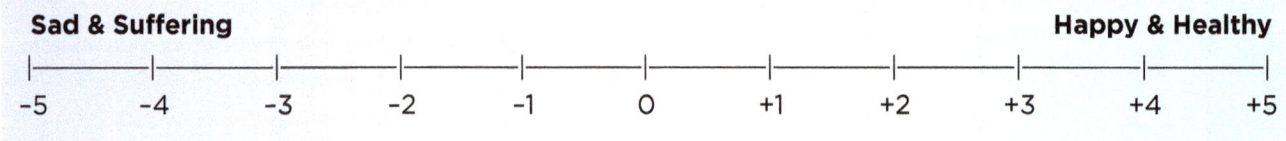

©2020 Dorothea Deley. www.GoodbyeDearDog.com

GUIDE SHEET #7 (continued)

PART 3 INSTRUCTIONS: Look at the Quality of Life score on page 66 and answer the following questions:

1. **Did your furbaby score in the "Sad & Suffering" end of the spectrum, the "Happy & Healthy" end, or somewhere in the middle?** _____
   _____
   _____
   _____

2. **Did your dog's score surprise you or was it about what you expected?** _____
   _____
   _____
   _____

3. **Would you like to talk to another family member or friend about your dog's score? What would you like to discuss with them?** _____
   _____
   _____
   _____

4. **What, if any, steps do you think you need to take next? Do you need to make an appointment with your vet?** _____
   _____
   _____
   _____

PART 4 INSTRUCTIONS: If your pet is still enjoying an acceptable quality of life, you may want to fill out this guide sheet again in a month. If s/he's not doing as well, you may want to fill it out in a week. Today's score acts as a baseline, and will help you notice any trends. Answer the following questions:

1. **When will you fill out this guide sheet again?**
   _____

2. **Would you like to receive monthly reminders by email to fill out your Dear Dog's Quality of Life guide sheet?**

   ☐ Yes, please remind me (sign up at the link in the "Get Support" box)

   ☐ No thanks

GET SUPPORT

Request Guide Sheet Reminder Email

WEBSITE: *GoodbyeDearDog.com/support*

KALI'S STORY

Struggling to Understand Kali's Quality of Life

As we navigated Kali's final months, Mike and I struggled to understand what was happening. Kali was our first dog together, our first dog as adults, and our first experience with an aging pet.

Our new vet wasn't much help either. He never once mentioned end-of-life options — no matter how sick Kali got or how much pain she was in.

It was all new to us.

Needing some kind of roadmap, I spent some time online researching this nebulous concept called "quality of life." Different veterinarians define it differently. I learned that some diseases can be managed so the dog continues to live — but with a radically diminished quality of life.

We definitely didn't want that for our Baby Bups! The problem, though, was we didn't know what constituted a "diminished" quality of life for Kali.

I was adrift in a sea of medicalese charts and checklists — not sure how any of it related to Kali.

After Kali's death I took all my research and created the Quality of Life tool in Guide Sheet #7. Then I filled it out retroactively for Kali.

Look at the next page to see how she would have scored during her last months of life.

Kali's Quality of Life Scores

PHYSICAL COMFORT

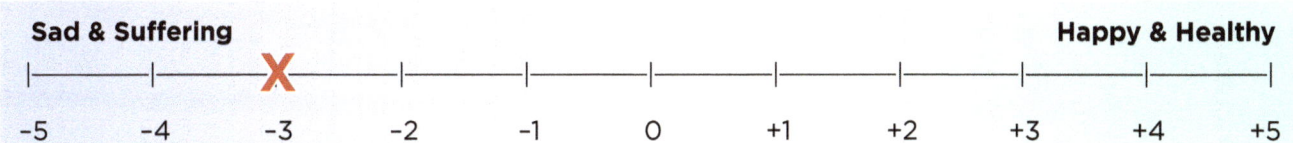

EMOTIONAL WELLBEING

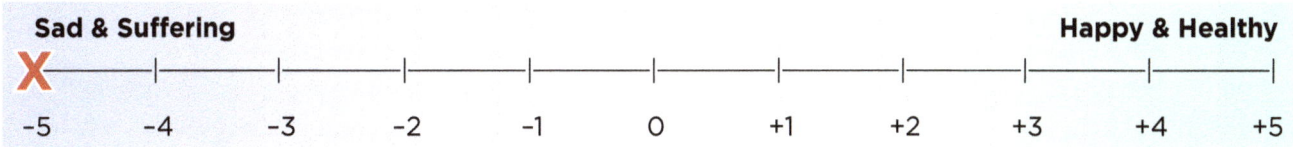

SOCIAL CONNECTION

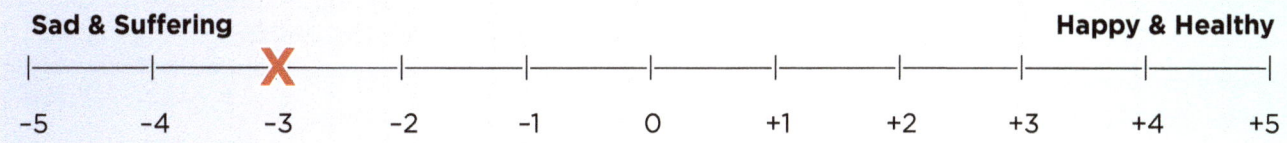

Seeing Now What I Couldn't Then

The numbers don't lie. When I add them together and divide by 3 for an average Happy or Hurting quality of life score, Kali would have had a −3.7.

QUALITY OF LIFE

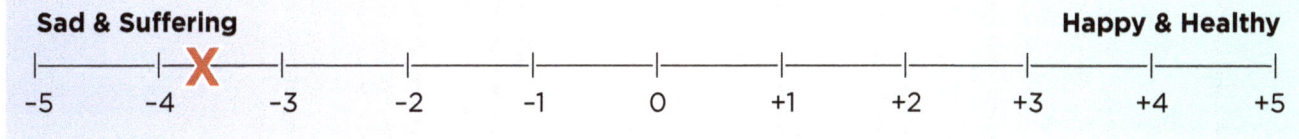

That's a very poor quality of life.

Looking back, it's pretty obvious that even with medical intervention, her diseases had progressed to a point where her quality of life was too compromised.

I am crying as I type this. Crying with sorrow that our girl suffered so much at the end. And crying with relief that we made the right decision to euthanize her.

Now I understand why many vets say, "It's better to euthanize a week too early than a day too late."

QUESTION

8

Has my Dear Dog given me a sign?

THE STORY OF MAGGIE

When Rory and Lea Molacek were little, their family adopted a playful mutt puppy and named her Maggie. The three girls grew up together, romping outside beneath the trees.

When Rory and Lea were teenagers, Maggie developed a tumor on her leg. No matter what the vet did, the tumor grew. Eventually it broke through the skin.

"Poor Maggie," says mom Gingy. "She had to wear a cone all the time to keep her from licking the ulceration."

Photo by Gingy Molacek

With each passing day the erupted tumor grew fouler and more painful. The vet said the only option was to amputate Maggie's leg. The Molaceks decided against it, though. Maggie was in her twilight years and they didn't want to put her through major surgery.

"One day we found Maggie outside under a tree," says Gingy. "She was in a nest of leaves, something she had never done before. It was clear to us she had made her deathbed."

The family decided together that it was time to put Maggie down. They found a vet clinic with a special cottage attached to it for a homier setting for euthanasia.

"We sat on the carpet and cried," Gingy says. "We held Maggie and loved her while the vet explained the procedure."

Maggie rolled over and let the girls rub her tummy one last time. She even thumped her tail a few times. The vet said that's because she still had some joy in her.

"In some ways that made it even harder," Gingy says, "because she was still Maggie, still loving us and letting us love her. But we knew — because of the deathbed she made — she was ready to go."

Why We Might Want A Sign

It can be a scary and lonely decision to euthanize our furbabies. It's natural to look for anything that might make this decision easier on us.

Here are common reasons we heard from Dog Parents that they wanted a "sign" from their Dear Dog that he was ready to die:

- ♥ Permission to end his life
- ♥ Reassurance that euthanasia was the right thing to do
- ♥ Relief of the responsibility of deciding on their own
- ♥ Peace of mind afterward that it was the right time

This is a good time to pause for a moment and remember our mantra:

> *"When I listen to my heart, I do good things.*
> *My heart is bigger than my hurt."*

SAY MANTRA

Put your hands over your heart and say aloud:

"When I listen to my heart, I do good things."

"My heart is bigger than my hurt."

What Our Dear Dogs Think about Death

Our Dear Dogs, while beloved members of our family, are not humans. They do not share our human worries or fears.

From our dogs' perspective, there's no right or wrong time to die. They're blessed to live in the present moment. They're not anxiously planning tomorrow or regretting what they did yesterday. They're just right here, right now.

Which is why we love them so much, right? It's also why they have no concept of — or fear of — dying. (That we're aware of, that is.)

Yes, there's a biological imperative programmed into them to survive, like all animals. But a survival instinct is different than a fear of death.

This is important because we tend to project our own worries, fears and feelings onto our furry friends. Your anxiousness about your pet's impending death does not mean she is actually concerned about her impending death.

WATCH THIS

Vicky Shares Jake's Story

WEBSITE: *GoodbyeDearDog.com/videos*

Three Ways our Dear Dogs Give Us Signs

Perhaps you too have heard that your dog will give you a sign when he's ready to go. I certainly had. But I had no clue what it meant.

How would Kali tell me she was ready to die? What kind of sign should I look for? Would I even know it if I saw it? What if I missed it, or worse, what if I misinterpreted it?

You may be asking yourself the same questions.

When Vicky Rees' lab Jake got sick, their vet told them they'd know it was time to let Jake go when he could no longer handle normal bodily functions like eating and going potty on his own.

"But," Vicky says, "the vet also said that because we have this 13-year relationship with this animal that we would know."

Like Vicky, you have a special bond with your Dear Dog. Which means I can't tell you what a sign from him will look like. Or what you'll feel in that moment. What I can tell you, though, is what to look for.

Photo by Ann Marie Gambino

"I sense my 14-year-old dog's time is coming," says Laura Lee Yates. "Venus is doing really well right now so I know it's a ways off. But I'm keeping an eye out for signs that she's ready to go."

Ways our Dear Dogs might communicate to us that they're ready to go:

1. A Sign May Come as an Unusual or Meaningful Action

Perhaps like the Molaceks' Maggie, your pup will give an obvious sign like making a deathbed. Or perhaps the sign will be subtler, like Kali staring at me while I read on the couch (see page 77).

You may see a sign when you least expect it and your guard is down. Or, you may see a sign when you give your pup your undivided attention for a moment.

2. A Sign May Come as A Physical, Emotional or Behavioral Change

All the questions and guide sheets leading up to this one are in fact "signs" from your Dear Dog.

Physical, emotional and social/behavioral changes are signals our Dear Dogs send us when they are suffering or in pain or distress. It's our responsibility as Dog Parents to recognize them as such.

3. A Sign May Not Come At All

I know you don't want to hear this, but you may not get a mystical or obvious sign from your Dear Dog at all. Just be open to that.

Instead of needing a signal from your Dear Dog that clearly says, "I'm ready to go," be open to simply *feeling* his **exhaustion**.

Feeling his **pain**.

Feeling his **suffering**.

Allow that to be your "sign."

> "People often say that the dog will 'tell you when it's time to go.' My opinion may not be a popular one, but I believe that when we wait for dogs to tell us, we have often waited too long. ... The day they lose one more pound and look more emaciated, can't get up to stand, or look at us pleadingly may well come after they have already suffered."
>
> — *Eileen Anderson, Dog Dementia Help & Support Website*

FILL OUT

Noticing Signs on page 76

WEBSITE:
GoodbyeDearDog.com/guidesheets

To Wait or Not To Wait for A Sign

None of us want to lose our Dear Dogs, and we definitely don't want to feel guilty afterward for ending their lives. Here's the catch, though — you will feel guilty regardless of when you euthanize. It's a natural reaction to ending the life of a beloved family member.

Several Dog Parents I interviewed, like Maggie's mom Gingy and Bailey's dad John, said they had seen the "signs" but didn't recognize them at the time. They feel they waited too long to euthanize, and regret putting their dogs through more suffering.

"When I look at the pictures of Maggie from before," says Gingy, "I can see now that her ears were flat and her tail rode low. She was in pain, but we told ourselves otherwise because she still wagged her tail and let us love her."

A few Dog Parents, like Jake's mom Vicky, saw the signs and felt they euthanized at the right time. And still they feel guilty.

As Vicky says, "You have guilt that you ended their life even though in your logical mind you know they were suffering and it was the best thing to do."

While you can't eliminate the guilt for ending your dog's life, you can eliminate the guilt for putting him through prolonged and needless suffering while you waited for a sign — or overlooked behavioral "signs."

As Gingy says, "A good question to ask yourself is, 'Who am I keeping my dog alive for, really?'"

A Picture Paints a Thousand Words

Mike and I found it helpful to look at old photos and videos of Kali. They reminded us what she loved to do when she felt well, and helped us see how unhappy she was at the end.

Guide Sheet #8 on the next page will help you do the same with your pup. To show you how it works, Mike and I filled it out for our other dog, Jenna.

THEN
SEPTEMBER 2013

NOW
DECEMBER 2019

Mike says, "Looking at this THEN photo of Jenna from when she was younger made me realize it was time to let her go. I could see the intelligence and joy in her eyes. I remembered who she was. That's gone now. She's not that dog anymore. There's just this thousand-yard stare in her eyes."

When I looked at the THEN photo I remembered what a sweet soul Jenna was. She was cuddly and playful. Everyone adored her and she loved their hugs! Now in Jenna's place there was a frightened dog who nipped at us, who paced the house for hours, who struggled in terror stuck in a corner.

It was time to say goodbye. Our sweet girl had left us already — we were still hanging on because we were afraid of letting her go. After a peaceful euthanasia at home, Jenna is with Kali now. ♥

For Kali, we'll use videos to show you how that works with Guide Sheet #8. They are viewable on our website — see the link in the "Watch This" box.

WATCH THIS

Kali's Then & Now

WEBSITE:
GoodbyeDearDog.com/videos

GUIDE SHEET #8

DOG'S NAME: _____   TODAY'S DATE: _____

Noticing Signs From Your Dear Dog

INSTRUCTIONS: Take a photo of your dog and print it out. Paste it in the "Now" box below and write in today's date. Find a photo of your dog from awhile ago when he was healthier — more "himself." Paste it in the "Then" box and write in the approximate month and year it was taken. Now look at your dog's two photos and answer the questions below. (If you have video from when your dog was well, you could shoot a video instead for a Then/Now comparison.)

THEN	**NOW**
Date: _____	Date: _____

1. **What is different between Then and Now?**
   _____
   _____

2. **How do you feel looking at these?**
   _____
   _____

3. **Look back at Guide Sheet #7 (pages 64-67). Could any of your dog's physical, emotional or social behavioral changes be seen as "signs" that he's ready to go?**
   _____
   _____
   _____

4. **Have you looked in your dog's eyes recently and felt a pang in your chest, tightness in your throat, or a hit in your gut? If so, what did that feel like?**
   _____
   _____
   _____

©2020 Dorothea Deley. www.GoodbyeDearDog.com

KALI'S STORY

Please Make it Better, Mom

I wanted a sign from Kali that euthanizing her was the right thing to do. A sign so obvious that I'd immediately feel at peace because I'd know beyond a doubt, with 100% certainty that it was time.

But it didn't work that way.

Instead, Kali and I shared a quiet moment that I chose to interpret as a "sign." No fireworks. No magic. Just the juxtaposition of the following two moments with my kid Kali.

Baby Bup's First Boo-Boo

One night when Kali was about a year old, she cut her paw while digging in our backyard. She hobbled in to the house and found me at my desk.

She held up her paw to show me her bloody wound. Her eyes seemed to say, "Look Mom, I'm hurt. Please make it better."

In that moment I felt like I truly became a "Dog Mom." This was my first baby's first boo-boo! And she trusted ME to help her!

I yelled for Mike and then ran to the bathroom for supplies. While I taped a maxi-pad to Kali's leg, Mike called the nearest emergency vet hospital to tell them we were on our way. We rushed out to the car and arrived at the hospital 20 minutes later.

They seemed to sense we were new Dog Parents, and were very sweet to us. After a quick exam, the vet assured us Kali's wound was superficial and would heal just fine with a couple of stitches.

The Boo-Boo I Couldn't Fix

Fast-forward 15 years. I was lying on the couch reading when I felt someone staring at me. I glanced up and saw Kali, who had been sleeping a moment before, looking right at me.

The look in her eyes made me catch my breath. In a flash, that memory of her first boo-boo as a baby came back to me. Just like all those years ago, her eyes seemed to say, "Look Mom, I'm hurt."

She was tired. She was in pain.

"Please make it better."

Only now there was only one way to make it better. Only one way to end her suffering. And that was to end my Baby Bups' life. In that moment, I became a Dog Mom in a deeper way than I ever imagined possible. Because I loved Kali, I would let her go.

Notes and Ideas

SECTION THREE:
Ask Yourself

"I think Bailey was ready to go, and it took me a long time to get there. The attachment was completely mine. I put Bailey through a year of unneeded pain and I don't like that."

— *John Thompson, Bailey's Dad*

QUESTION

9 How is caring for my Dear Dog affecting my family and me?

THE STORY OF JAKE

When Vicky Rees' sons were young, her family adopted a rambunctious yellow lab puppy. They named him "Jake" and he fit right in.

Jake grew into a protective playmate for the kids and a buddy for artist/stay-at-home mom Vicky. "He was a sweet dog. He was always there," she says. "And he was the only guy in our house that actually listened to me!"

When Jake was 13, he struggled getting up and down the stairs. Gradually he started losing control of his hind legs as arthritis paralyzed his spine.

Photo by Vicky Rees

That's when Vicky's family realized Jake was coming to the end of his life.

"We asked the vet how we would know when it was time to let Jake go," Vicky says. "She told us if he can't get up and walk for two or three days, or if he's not eating and drinking, or not evacuating his bowels like he's supposed to — you know, normal functions for a healthy dog — then it's time."

WATCH THIS

Vicky Shares Jake's Story

WEBSITE: GoodbyeDearDog.com/ videos

During Jake's final weeks Vicky became his primary caregiver. In the end, she had to carry her 80-pound buddy outside to go potty.

"By the third day he had a lot of edema," she says. "He was panting a lot. He was really miserable. We knew it was time."

She's cared for elderly human family members before too, and says she experienced similar feelings after Jake's death as she did with her human family member's passing. "In addition to all the grief, once they're gone, you're also relieved because you can finally relax. But you also feel guilty — it feels selfish."

It's been several years since Jake's death and Vicky finds herself crying telling his story. "Still gets me every time," she says. "Jake was such a great dog."

Caregiving for Our Dear Dogs Is Hard

We've been focusing on your Dear Dog up to this point. Now it's time to focus on you — what you've been feeling and what you need.

Initially I hadn't even thought of a caregiver question. Like Vicky mentioned, it seemed ... selfish somehow? Of course we're going to take care of our furbabies!

And then, as I talked to more and more Dog Parents, this question came up. A lot.

Not only were they worrying about their dogs, they were also raising kids or caring for aging relatives or keeping their marriages afloat or running a busy household or launching a new business or working to support their families.

Not to mention trying to squeeze in time for themselves!

In other words, they had other people and obligations to consider in addition to their furbaby. And you probably do too. At the very least you have your own health to consider.

Burnout is a serious consequence of long-term caregiving for any family member — human or canine. And burnout takes months, sometimes longer, to recover from.

So in addition of thinking about your doggie, I need you to think about yourself right now too.

Caring for a sick family member — dogs included — is stressful. In addition to the emotional toll, caregiving for our Dear Dogs can be physically and financially draining, and negatively affect our relationships.

Let's explore each area separately.

> "Caregiving for our pets is as stressful as caregiving for our human family members."
>
> — *Dr. Mary Beth Spitznagel, Kent State University*

Emotional Toll of Caring for Our Sick Dogs

Mary Beth Spitznagel, PhD, of Kent State University, teamed up with veterinarians at two animal hospitals in Kent, Ohio. Together they conducted the first-ever study of pet caregivers.

They interviewed 600 people who were caring for their sick or dying pets. Here's what they found, according to Spitznagel:

> *"It turns out that the effects of caregiving for a sick pet — stress, anxiety, depression, low quality of life — are in many ways similar to what we see in a person caring for a sick family member, for example, a parent with dementia."*

Spitznagel and her colleagues found that pet caregivers often experienced distressing feelings. Are you experiencing any of the following related to caregiving for your Dear Dog?

- ♥ Stressed, overwhelmed, too much to do and not enough time
- ♥ Angry or strained around your sick dog or other loved ones
- ♥ Fearful about the future
- ♥ Anxiety and/or depression
- ♥ Uncertain about which treatments to choose
- ♥ Guilt about wanting to do a better job
- ♥ Loneliness, less social interaction with friends, shut down or distant
- ♥ Weepy or despondent
- ♥ Detached from activities usually cared about before

Thinking back to Kali's final months I realize I felt emotionally "out of it" much of the time. Whether my feeling spacey was from being emotionally drained or perhaps even a coping mechanism, I can't say.

I was relieved, though, to read Dr. Spitznagel and colleagues' above list. Apparently what I was feeling was normal! I just didn't know it at the time.

Spitznagel wants pet caregivers to realize it's stressful, and to acknowledge how caregiving may be taking a toll on their lives. She reminds us, "Acknowledging the stress doesn't mean they love their pet any less."

How is caring for your Dear Dog affecting your emotional wellbeing?

READ MORE

Pet Caregiving Study

WEBSITE: GoodbyeDearDog.com/resources

Physical Toll of Caregiving for Our Sick Dogs

The biggest physical impact I experienced while caring for Kali was exhaustion. This seems almost universal among the dog owners we interviewed. You're either up multiple times a night helping your pet, or laying in bed wide awake worrying about her.

Other physical symptoms I experienced were upset stomach and headaches — definitely stress-related. I also got sick more often than usual with common ailments like colds and flu. No doubt my immune system was compromised because of not getting enough rest. Plus being sad can depress our immunity.

To be honest, sometimes having a cold and getting to spend a couple days in bed was almost a respite from the responsibility of caring for Kali.

What are you experiencing physically that may be related to caregiving for your Dear Dog?

GET SUPPORT

Share your feelings with other Dog Parents.

WEBSITE: GoodbyeDearDog.com/support

> "It was amazing to me how much time and energy I spent taking care of Jake. You don't realize how much time you're spending nurturing and worrying about them. Once they're gone you can breathe again."
>
> — *Vicky Rees, Jake's Mom*

Financial Toll of Caring for Our Sick Dogs

Caregiving for our dogs can be expensive. Treating chronic diseases like diabetes or kidney failure, or terminal illnesses like cancer, can cost between $1,000 – $10,000 or more over the long haul.

Here are how several Dog Parents faced the financial question.

RACHEL MENDOZA

A part-time dental assistant, Rachel also cares for her four children and 10-year-old black lab named Missy. Years ago, when Rachel and her husband first adopted Missy, they sat down and had a frank conversation. They agreed their children come first, so they made a budget for their Dear Dog. They now know how much they can afford to spend on Missy's medical care when the time comes. "Missy's in pretty good shape right now," Rachel says, "but I know in the not-too-distant future me and my husband will need to make a decision."

RYAN BIGGS

Another Dog Parent with children, Ryan, chose to start a special savings account for his dog. "Every family member contributes," he says. "Turns out to be a good way to teach kids about saving and charitable giving."

JANET AMADOR

A high school teacher with two daughters, Janet's family had to make a hard decision when their 10-year-old Miniature Schnauzer developed pancreatitis. "The vet could have saved her but the cost would have been upward of $6,000," Janet says. "It was very difficult making a decision based solely on dollars and cents. It's been over a year and I still wish we could have kept her."

> "We had to put our 10-year-old Miniature Schnauzer down due to pancreatitis. The vet could have saved her but the cost would have been upward of $6,000."
>
> — *Janet Amador, Dog Parent*

Like the Dog Parents above, money may be an important consideration for you. I know it was for Mike and me. But we learned something else after our experience with Kali: Both Mike and I agree that any treatment that prolongs our dogs' lives while also prolonging their suffering is not an option, even if we can afford it.

How much are you willing — and able — to spend on your Dear Dog's care?

Relationship Toll of Caring for Our Sick Dogs

Taking care of our sick dogs can also negatively affect our relationships.

Your caregiving duties might take up so much of your day that you no longer have time to spend with friends or family. You may be stuck at home a lot more than usual, only leaving for work, school, groceries and vet visits. This isolation and lack of social contact might leave you feeling lonely and strain your relationships.

Or you and your family members may disagree about your pup's care, arguing over decisions like which veterinary treatment to pursue and how much to spend. This discord might leave you withdrawing from each other.

If you find yourself irritable and short with others — from family members to strangers — take a moment to notice what's happening. More than likely it's not about the other person at all. Instead it might be about you and what's going on with your Dear Dog.

How is caregiving for your Dear Dog affecting your social relationships with other loved ones?

Adobe Stock Image

HOW TO KNOW YOU NEED A BREAK

If you find yourself overwhelmed, irritable or exhausted, pause and ask:

AM I ...

Hungry?
Angry?
Lonely?
Tired or Sick?

If so, you need to **HALT**!

It's time to take care of yourself:

♥ Eat if you're hungry.

♥ Take a deep breath if you're angry.

♥ Call a friend if you're lonely.

♥ Rest if you're tired or sick.

SECTION THREE: ASK YOURSELF

TAKE A BREAK

Caregiving is hard. Take time for yourself.

Caregiving is Hard — Take a Break

Are you caring for a sick or elderly dog? Here are several suggestions for ways to support yourself:

♥ Recognize that caregiving for your Dear Dog is stressful and probably taking a toll on your life. That is not a failure on your part — that is normal for everyone.

♥ Ask other family members to help with some of the caregiving duties.

♥ Ask a family member or close friend to watch your doggo while you take an hour or two off for yourself. Go do something relaxing and replenishing without guilt, like going for a long walk or meeting a friend for lunch.

♥ Talk with a therapist, grief counselor, pet bereavement support group, or other mental health professional. In addition to feeling stressed, you may be experiencing "anticipatory grief." A mental health professional can help.

♥ Consider if it's time to say goodbye to your Dear Dog.

♥ Feel free to share your caregiving feelings and experiences with other Dog Parents on our forum. Sometimes just knowing other people are out there going through a similar struggle can make all the difference.

First, though, fill out Guide Sheet #9 to understand how caregiving may be affecting you and your family.

FILL OUT

Caring for My Dear Dog on next page

WEBSITE:
GoodbyeDearDog.com/ guidesheets

GUIDE SHEET #9

DOG'S NAME: _____ TODAY'S DATE: _____

How Is Caring for My Dear Dog Affecting Me?

INSTRUCTIONS: To help you think about how your Dear Dog's illness might be affecting you and your family, circle **YES** or **NO** for each of the following and then answer the questions below:

YES   NO   **Are the demands of caring for my dog draining me emotionally?**

Am I "out of it" much of the time? Weepy or despondent? Shut down, distant and detached from people and activities I usually care about? Irritable and snippy with others? Am I anxious, in a constant state of stress and worry?

YES   NO   **Are my dog caregiving duties wearing me down physically?**

Am I tired most of time? Am I getting sick more often? Experiencing headaches? Upset stomach? Or other stress-related physical ailments?

YES   NO   **Are the financial costs of veterinary care more than I can afford?**

Have I exceeded my "budget" for my pet's care? Am I going into debt or not covering basic bills or spending money earmarked for other things? Are family members and I disagreeing about how much money to spend treating and/or caring for our dog?

YES   NO   **Is my caregiving straining my social relationships with friends and family?**

Am I so busy caregiving that I no longer spend time with friends or loved ones? Am I stuck at home, only leaving for work, school, groceries and vet visits? Do I feel lonely? Am I fighting with family about veterinary treatments, including euthanasia?

Circle the areas of your life affected by caregiving:

EMOTIONAL   PHYSICAL   FINANCIAL   SOCIAL

What can you do today to take care of yourself, even if it's just for five minutes?

_____
_____
_____
_____
_____
_____
_____
_____
_____
_____

©2020 Dorothea Deley. www.GoodbyeDearDog.com

KALI'S STORY

Caregiving Was Harder Than We Realized

I don't think Mike and I understood just how stressful caring for a sick dog was going to be. For almost two months, we:

- ♥ Took Kali to the vet every other week to have fluid drained from her abdomen.
- ♥ Gave her multiple medications that had to be carefully timed throughout the day.
- ♥ Picked her up when she collapsed.
- ♥ Wiped her off when she went potty on herself — sometimes in the middle of the night.
- ♥ Hand-fed her when she was too weak to stand up to eat.

Each morning we woke up exhausted, wondering if Kali had made it through the night.

We spent our days watching her suffer and not being able to help. We worried she'd go into cardiac arrest and need to be rushed to an emergency vet. Or we'd be gone when it happened and she'd die alone in pain.

Caregiving Strained Our Relationship

Dreading the inevitable loss of her day after day strained our relationship. This dread is called "anticipatory grief" and is normal, but I didn't know that then.

We bickered over the cost of her care, disagreed about when to put her down, and argued about which treatments to pursue. We grew distant in a way that surprised — even scared — us. A distance that, in all honesty, took months to repair after her death.

I was afraid of not just losing Kali, but of losing Mike too.

I felt awkward in social settings, afraid I'd burst into tears at any moment. Over time my pleasure in life dimmed, like a perpetually overcast day.

After we euthanized our Baby Bups, I felt relief mixed with sorrow. It was over — the worrying, stress and fear. Now we could move on to the next phase: grieving.

QUESTION 10

What does my heart tell me to do for my Dear Dog?

THE STORY OF SIDNEY

Photo by Michelle Brunson

Gustavo Brett got a call from the local animal shelter where he volunteered. An injured pit bull puppy needed a place to heal and recuperate before the shelter could put her up for adoption.

Gustavo and his then girlfriend, Michelle, brought the puppy home and named her Sidney. "Sidney was intense," Gustavo says, "but crazy sweet, too." They fell in love with her and eventually adopted her.

Sidney's intensity led to many brushes with death. Once she leapt out a second story window to chase after a skunk. Another time she dove into an irrigation culvert and reappeared a mile downstream. Her most epic exploit, though, was the time she got into a fight with an angry raccoon.

In the end, it was cancer that Sidney couldn't overcome.

Before they knew she was sick, Gustavo sensed something was wrong. "There were moments when I was watching her and I started getting this strong intuitive feeling, like she's dying" he says. "I'd start to cry and tell her how much I love her and how I was her Papa."

About seven weeks later one of her back legs swelled up: osteosarcoma.

The vet offered to amputate 8-year-old Sidney's leg but Gustavo decided against it. A few months earlier she had ruptured a spinal disk and hadn't fully recovered. "We'd go walking in the field behind our house, and Sid would flop down on the grass and just lay there looking around instead of continuing our walk."

Gustavo says he just knew it was time to let Sid go.

He opted for at-home euthanasia and burial. A close friend helped him dig a grave in the field where Sidney loved to run. Friends stopped by to say goodbye and give Sidney one last hug. And then the vet came over.

"Sid was laying in the sunshine," Gustavo says. "She wasn't in pain. Her mom, Michelle, was there. It was a good passing."

WATCH THIS

Gustavo Shares Sidney's Story

WEBSITE: *GoodbyeDearDog.com/ videos*

SECTION THREE: ASK YOURSELF

Seeking Guidance from Head & Heart

Euthanizing our Dear Dogs may be the most loving thing we ever do for them.

It's hard to wrap our minds around that paradox, though, isn't it?

> "'I woke up one day and I knew it was time' … might be the most common mode of decision-making I hear about. This much certainty some pet owners arrive at on their own has an amazing way of granting peace."
>
> — *Dr. Patty Khuly, PetMD Veterinarian*

As humans, we're both blessed — and cursed — with having rational minds, which I call our "head." We can rationalize ourselves in to and out of almost any decision in the blink of an eye. It's confusing! Which decision is the right decision?

And when you're trying to make such an important decision like ending your Dear Dog's life, this confusion can be discouraging.

One way to find clarity when our rational mind fails us is to listen to what I call our "heart." Albert Einstein called it our "intuitive mind." You may call it your:

- ♥ Intuition
- ♥ Gut Instinct
- ♥ Inner Wisdom
- ♥ Divine Connection
- ♥ God
- ♥ Life Force
- ♥ Spirit
- ♥ Inner Compass
- ♥ North Star
- ♥ Love

Whatever you choose to call your personal source of guidance is up to you.

Many Dog Parents we talked to, like Gustavo, said that listening to their hearts ultimately helped them decide when it was time to euthanize their dogs.

Our hearts don't lie the way our heads sometimes can. Instead, the challenge with our heart is hearing it at all.

Our hope is that this last question helps you hear your heart too so you can make this difficult decision with love and clarity.

> "The rational mind is a faithful servant. The intuitive mind is a precious gift."
>
> —Albert Einstein

Our Hearts Know the Way

Just the other day Mike said, "I can't imagine anything worse than having to end your beloved family member's life, but that's what we had to do because we love Kali."

Ending your loved one's life is not a purely rational decision. How could it be? It is also an emotional decision because love is an emotion.

Once I let go of my desperate researching and ruminating — the "head" approach — and let myself really feel Kali's pain, I could finally hear what my heart was telling me. The choice was obvious.

It took me much too long to get there, though. By then I was exhausted and Kali was miserable. I want to save you and your Dear Dog the suffering. So I created a guided visualization for Guide Sheet #10 to help you hear your heart.

I understand guided visualizations may not be for everyone. Still, I encourage to you listen to the audio one time — it's just five minutes long. Once you've listened to it you can do it on your own without the audio. Or you can decide once was enough.

Photo by Ian Smaller

WHERE DO YOU FEEL LOVE?

We talk a lot about listening to your heart in this question. If you're not sure where this internal source of knowing is, or how to get in touch with it, here's a hint:

It's the place where you feel love for your Dear Dog.

I feel it in my upper chest. Where do you feel it?

FILL OUT

Hearing My Heart on next page

WEBSITE: GoodbyeDearDog.com/guidesheets

GUIDE SHEET #10

DOG'S NAME: _____ TODAY'S DATE: _____

Hearing My Heart Meditation & Affirmation

MEDITATION INSTRUCTIONS: Set aside 5 or 10 uninterrupted minutes to listen to our **guided meditation audio** (see link in "Listen Up" box). Or if you prefer, do this on your own: Sit quietly and close your eyes. Take a couple of deep breaths. Place both hands over your heart and call up a favorite memory of your Dear Dog. Spend a few moments reliving it until your chest fills with love and you find yourself smiling. Then answer these questions:

1. **When you thought of a happy memory of your Dear Dog, what came up?**
   _____
   _____
   _____

2. **When you thought of your dog in the present, what came up — a word? image? feeling? nothing?**
   _____
   _____
   _____

3. **What does your heart tell you to do?**
   _____
   _____
   _____

AFFIRMATION INSTRUCTIONS: Write the following phrase on an index card or sticky note: *When I listen to my heart, I do good things.* At least once a day put your hands on your heart and repeat the words aloud three times. Try looking into your own eyes in a mirror when you repeat the phrase. Place the card somewhere where you will see it everyday.

LISTEN UP

Heart Meditation

WEBSITE:
GoodbyeDearDog.com/meditation

©2020 Dorothea Deley. www.GoodbyeDearDog.com

KALI'S STORY

Unexpected Gifts of Listening to My Heart

I had lost people and pets before. Why did this time with Kali feel so different? This time it was my responsibility. This time it was my decision.

When I first accepted that Kali's health would never get better, it felt like I was betraying her. I even felt betrayed by love. Love isn't supposed to hurt this much!

Reliving all this with you reminds me to pause and repeat our mantra:

> *"When I listen to my heart, I do good things. My heart is bigger than my hurt."*

My heart, ultimately, guided me when my head couldn't "figure out" what to do. My heart let me see the most loving decision of all was to let Kali go. I think deep down I already knew what my heart was trying to tell me. Perhaps that's why I kept my head so busy with research and rumination.

Camping For the Last Time

Remember the final camping trip I decided to take Kali on because my heart told me to? It offered some surprising gifts. I wanted to share a few with you to hopefully encourage you to listen to your heart as well. Taking Kali:

- ♥ Gave us a chance to share one last camping trip as a family. We made special — albeit bittersweet — memories with her.
- ♥ Helped us accept the reality of Kali's health. On that trip there was no denying how sick she was.
- ♥ Created a precious place to return to later to remember Kali. It was healing to stand in the canyon creek the following year with Mike and Jenna, sharing stories and laughing, our tears floating away in the current.

We had three more months with Kali after that trip. We didn't know that at the time, of course. But because I listened to my heart we had this special time together.

Notes and Ideas

> "Dogs show us the true meaning of unconditional love. All we can do in this life when they're gone is continue sharing that love with others."
>
> — *Jim Howden, Luna & Mirdog's Dad*

SECTION FOUR:
Making Your Decision

 # Bringing all 10 questions together

THE STORY OF MOJITO

Photo by David Beer

When Nicöle Beer was a single 20-something, she adopted a long-haired Chihuahua. She named him Mojito, and for the next 11 years he was by her side through life's challenges and joys.

"When Momo was happy he'd do a silly prancing walk that made me laugh," Nicöle says. "And whenever I was sad or sick he'd press his little body next to mine."

A few years after Nicöle married David, they welcomed their daughter, Maddy, into the family. At first Momo was jealous of the new baby. "He would sit on Maddy's chairs or my lap so she couldn't," Nicöle says. "He'd even take her toys!" Eventually Maddy and Momo became best buddies.

When Mojito was nine, he was diagnosed with a heart murmur. Medication helped at first, but then his health deteriorated rapidly. "He started losing control of his bowels and fainting," Nicöle says.

One day she came home to find Mojito howling in pain. The emergency vet suspected a ruptured spinal disk, but needed an MRI to confirm before doing surgery.

An ultrasound revealed Mojito's heart was leaking blood into the surrounding sac. He'd need to have the blood drained through a needle inserted into his chest before they could anesthetize him for the MRI or surgery. He'd have to endure this uncomfortable procedure regularly for the rest of his life.

Overwhelmed, Nicöle called Mojito's primary vet. "I trusted her," Nicöle says. "She said dogs don't survive the draining of the blood from the heart sac for long. She had done it for a lab who made it six weeks, and with a small dog like Mojito, facing surgery, she didn't think he'd live very long."

Suddenly Nicöle had to make a very hard decision. "He was in terrible pain and we either needed to move forward with the blood draining, MRI and surgery or put him down."

She chose euthanasia. The family spent their final few hours together at home, outside on the lawn in the sunshine. Nicöle cradled Mojito in her lap while Maddy petted him and quietly said goodbye.

First, A Hug

Answering the 10 questions in this guidebook took tremendous courage. Please take a moment to:

- ♥ acknowledge yourself for being a kind and thoughtful Dog Parent;
- ♥ feel some compassion for yourself and the difficult situation you're in; and
- ♥ treat yourself with love and tenderness, like you would treat your pup.

You care deeply for your Dear Dog. That is why this decision is so hard.

Kind, loving people like you restore my faith in humanity, and I want you to know that Mike and I, and all the other Dog Parents who helped with this guidebook, are sending you an encouraging hug.

You are part of an openhearted, brokenhearted family of Dog Parents. We're courageous enough to love . . . and our lives are so much richer for having known our Dear Dogs.

READ MORE

Relief is Natural

WEBSITE:
GoodbyeDearDog.com/resources

Benefits of Deciding to Euthanize

It may be hard to imagine right now, but there are definitely benefits to deciding to euthanize. Until you do, you may be plagued by the questions below. I know I was with Kali.

These questions will keep you up at night and invade your thoughts during the day. That may already be happening to you.

- ♥ When will my Dear Dog die?
- ♥ How will my Dear Dog die?
- ♥ Where will my Dear Dog die?
- ♥ Will my Dear Dog's death be painful or peaceful?
- ♥ Will my Dear Dog die all alone or will I be there?
- ♥ Will my Dear Dog be scared?
- ♥ Can I cover the costs of my Dear Dog's death?
- ♥ Will I get to say goodbye to my Dear Dog?

> "I wish that I would have put Gracie down much earlier. You need to be aware of when they're ready to go and don't wait too long."
>
> — *Marilyn Colter, Gracie's Mom*

The benefit of deciding to euthanize your dog is that you get answers to the above questions. You may even feel relieved — Mike and I certainly did. Vicky did. John did too. Most Dog Parents do. It's perfectly normal so please don't feel bad about it.

You might find oncology veterinarian Dr. Alice Villalobos's article, "Relief is a Natural Component of Grief," reassuring. See a link to it in the "Read More" box.

It's Hard to Let Go — We Know

If you know it's time to let go, but you're unable to euthanize your Dear Dog because you're afraid of saying goodbye, afraid of the heartbreak and loneliness you'll feel afterward — we get it. We've all been there.

But that's not a good enough reason to keep your pet alive.

We'd all prefer it if our beloved companions could die peacefully and naturally at home, preferably in their sleep. But a natural death isn't always peaceful. It can be painful and traumatic, and distressing to watch.

If you're putting off making a decision, know that choosing to do "nothing" is actually a decision.

Think about the stories you've read in this guidebook from dog owners who felt they waited too long to euthanize their dogs. These Dog Parents bravely shared their painful stories with you because they want you to benefit from their experiences.

It's Time to Decide

If you haven't made a decision yet, now is the time.

We have one final guide sheet for you on the next page. It brings together all 10 questions in this guidebook onto one page so you can truly see the "big picture."

By this point in our guidebook you may have already decided it's time to euthanize. If so, feel free to skip the Guide Sheet #11 and jump to the "Once You've Decided" section on page 103.

FILL OUT
Making a Decision on next page

WEBSITE:
GoodbyeDearDog.com/ guidesheets

> "'Going to sleep and not waking up' is what medical euthanasia provides, Mother Nature generally does not."
> — Drs. Mary Gardner & Dani McVety, *Lap of Love Veterinary Hospice*

GUIDE SHEET #11

DOG'S NAME: _____ TODAY'S DATE: _____

Bringing All 10 Questions Together to Make a Decision

INSTRUCTIONS: Now that you've worked through all the questions individually, let's bring them together on one page so you can see the big picture. Looking back over the most recent guide sheets you've filled out, answer the questions below:

QUESTION 1: **What is my Dear Dog's prognosis according to our vet?** (pages 17-18)

_____

_____

QUESTION 2: **Have I seen a vet specialist and what did they say?** (page 27)

_____

_____

QUESTION 3: **Is my Dear Dog in physical pain?** (page 36)
☐ Yes   ☐ No

QUESTION 4: **Does my Dear Dog still enjoy favorite activities?** (page 44-45)
☐ Yes   ☐ No

QUESTION 5: **Is my Dear Dog withdrawing socially?** (pages 50)
☐ Yes   ☐ No

QUESTION 6: **Has my Dear Dog's personality or emotional state changed?** (pages 56-57)
☐ Yes   ☐ No

QUESTION 7: **How is my Dear Dog's quality of life?** (pages 64-67)
☐ Happy & Healthy   ☐ Sad & Suffering

QUESTION 8: **Has my Dear Dog given me a sign that s/he's ready to go?** (page 76)
☐ Yes   ☐ No

QUESTION 9: **Is caring for my Dear Dog negatively affecting me emotionally, physically, socially, and/or financially?** (page 87)
☐ Yes   ☐ No

QUESTION 10: **What does my heart tell me to do for my Dear Dog?** (page 92)

_____

_____

MY DECISION: **Based on my answers above, is it time to say goodbye to my Dear Dog?**
☐ Yes   ☐ No

©2020 Dorothea Deley. www.GoodbyeDearDog.com

KALI'S STORY

The Gift of Finally Making a Decision

Before we decided it was time to euthanize Kali, Mike and I knew her time with us was coming to a close one way or the other. We just didn't know when or how, so we lived in a constant state of worry.

Making the decision to euthanize her meant we could finally know some of the unknowns that had distressed us for months. Now we had control over the situation. We made these big decisions:

- ♥ Kali would die on July 23, 2015.
- ♥ She would die peacefully at home.
- ♥ She'd be surrounded by her family.
- ♥ A local mobile veterinarian who reminded us of our vet back in Colorado would come to our house to euthanize Kali.
- ♥ She'd die from a two-injection barbiturate euthanasia process, considered the most humane.
- ♥ Extended family would have a chance to come over and say goodbye to Kali if they wanted to beforehand.
- ♥ We could tell friends our plans and start to get the support we had been denying ourselves while we lived in the limbo of trying to figure out what to do.
- ♥ After Kali's death, we would have about an hour alone with her before we drove her to the pet cemetery for cremation.
- ♥ We would have Kali cremated alone so we could have her ashes, which we would keep at home.
- ♥ We knew how much Kali's euthanasia and cremation would cost, so we set aside that amount from our budget.
- ♥ We would get to spend a special last day with our Baby Bups doing some of her favorite activities, like riding in the car.

The day before Kali's euthanasia, we took her for a drive around the three-mile loop we used to walk in our neighborhood. We rolled the windows down and drove slowly, letting her take it all in one last time.

KALI'S STORY, continued

READ MORE

Our Special Last Day with Kali

WEBSITE:
GoodbyeDearDog.com/resources

Knowing Lifted a Burden

As heartbreaking as the decision to euthanize Kali was, it felt like a burden had lifted. Now we knew what was going to happen, we knew when and where, and we knew who and how.

We also knew it would be a peaceful passing for her — something that was important to us.

There was some comfort in that.

The biggest blessing of all, though, was having time to say goodbye. Many dog owners we interviewed did not get that opportunity. We are forever grateful we did.

SECTION FIVE:
Once You've Decided

"If you can love everyone around you unconditionally ... and if you can always find contentment just where you are ... then you're probably a dog!"

— *Dr. Shauna Shapiro, clinical psychologist, "The Power of Mindfulness" TEDx Talk*

Making end-of-life plans

THE STORY OF BETTY

When Cindy Smith got a new job across the country, she worried about her elderly dog Betty. Betty was incontinent, deaf, arthritic, and required a lot of care. Would Betty survive the upheaval of a move?

Would she adapt to the new house? Colder weather? A new routine?

Excited about the new life awaiting her, Cindy also felt torn. "I was moving to new city where I didn't know anyone. I really wanted Betty with me for the move so I wouldn't be all alone. But I knew the move would be hard on Betty."

With a heavy heart, Cindy decided it would be kinder to euthanize Betty before the move.

"That way Betty was at home when she died," Cindy says. "I wanted her to feel safe. And I wanted our friends and family there for both of us. Betty died in familiar surroundings surrounded by people she knew and loved."

Making the Arrangements — We're Here to Help

Now that you've decided to euthanize your Dear Dog, it's time to set the date and make the arrangements.

Please know you are not alone. We are here for you.

We suggest you take the following steps in preparation for your pup's passing:

1. Decide When Is Best For You
2. Choose Vet and Location of Euthanasia
3. Decide How to Handle Remains
4. Accept Events May Not Go As Planned
5. Seek Support Before and After
6. Trust Yourself and Your Decision

We will walk you through these steps in the next few pages. When we're done you will have an End-of-Life Plan on page 117 for your Dear Dog and people in place to support you.

Remember You Gave Yourself Permission

Before we go any further, let's revisit your Permission Slip from page 6. Take a moment to re-read it. Let it sink it.

Take a deep breath.

Now let's talk through each of the above steps.

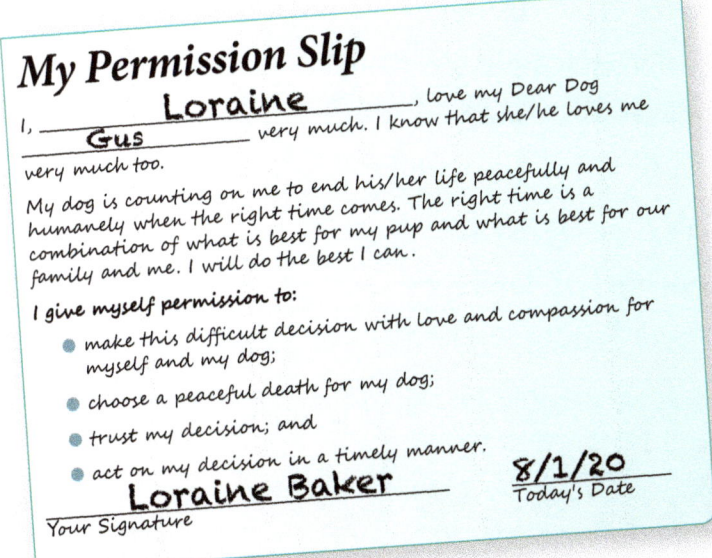

1. Decide When Is Best for You

In addition to when is best for your Dear Dog, consider when is best for you and your family.

Here are some of the situations Dog Parents we talked to grappled with:

- ♥ Should we wait to put her down until after Christmas, after everyone comes home for the holidays and has a chance to say goodbye?
- ♥ Should we wait to put him down until the kids are back in school so they're more distracted, or do it before school starts so they have a few days to grieve and process their loss?
- ♥ Should we do it now before we go on our big trip to Hawaii and she has to suffer through being boarded in a kennel for three weeks?

It's okay to ask yourself these kinds of questions. They're not callous or selfish — they're honest and important.

Sometimes being kind to ourselves is a kindness to our Dear Dogs, too.

Include Loved Ones If You Can — and Want

Let close friends and extended family members know your plan. See if they would like to say goodbye to your Dear Dog a few days beforehand at your home. Give them a specific window of time that is convenient for you.

If this becomes too complicated in any way, don't do it. And only invite those folks who won't stress you out! Remember, this is a time to think first and foremost about what you and your Dear Dog need.

"We were considering having Jake euthanized at home. We discussed what that would entail financially, logistically and experientially. We decided that if we all went to the vet with him together, that it would be just as peaceful a passing for him — and for us too — as if we had done it here at the house."

— Vicky Rees, Jake's Mom

2. Choose Vet and Location

When it comes to choosing where to have your dog's euthanasia done and who will do it, you might want to consider the following factors:

- ♥ What type of euthanasia process does the vet use?
- ♥ Are owners allowed to be present or not?
- ♥ How much does it cost?
- ♥ Do we have a relationship with the vet?

ASK VET
About Euthanasia Services on page 116

There are two types of pet euthanasia:

SINGLE-INJECTION PROCESS

Intravenous injection (IV) of a barbiturate like pentobarbital, an anti-seizure medication, at an overdose level. The pet is awake during this procedure. Some vets will take your pet away to shave their leg and insert the IV catheter, then bring them back to the exam room where you are as they administer the drug. This process usually costs less than the two-injection process below because it does not include a sedative.

TWO-INJECTION PROCESS

Injection of a sedative at a dose that makes the pet unconscious (like before surgery). Then, a second injection of a barbiturate at an overdose level is given. Some vets use separate syringes while others prefer an IV. Once the first anesthetic is administered, the pet is asleep for the second, lethal injection.

In both the single- and two-injection process, it is the overdose of the barbiturate that slows and then stops the dog's heart. Blood pressure drops and blood circulation decreases. Breathing slows and then stops. Finally, circulation of oxygen to the brain stops and your pet dies. In both cases, death usually happens rapidly.

See "What to Expect During and After Euthanasia" on the next page before deciding which process is best for you and your Dear Dog.

If you opt for an in-clinic euthanasia, request an appointment during a slower, quieter time, like early morning or end of day. If possible, make a Friday or weekend appointment when you won't have to go back to work the next day and your kids won't have to go back to school.

What to Expect During and After Euthanasia

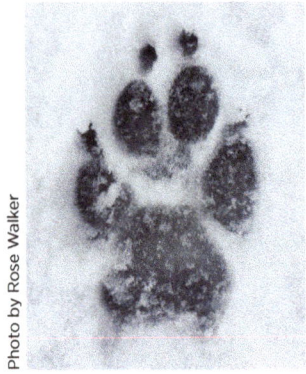
Photo by Rose Walker

When we euthanized Kali I didn't know what to expect. I had never been present for a pet euthanasia before. The not knowing made the experience even harder.

For this guidebook, I did research and asked our current vet what she's seen happen when she's euthanized pets. I include that information here.

Just to let you know, this section may be difficult to read.

What to Expect Immediately After Euthanasia

- ♥ Your pet may appear to take a sudden "breath" after death. This is just air escaping the lungs.

- ♥ Some pets may move or cry out after death — both of which are involuntary muscle contractions as the brain shuts down. Some vets will cover your pet's face just in case this happens since it can be upsetting to see. This is less likely with the two-injection process.

- ♥ Most pets lose bladder and/or bowel control upon dying.

These same sort of physiological responses happen with humans immediately after death as well. They are natural and do not mean that your pet suffered or that the vet did a poor job.

What to Expect A Few Hours After Euthanasia

- ♥ Within a couple hours after death rigor mortis sets in. This can be hard for Dog Parents to see, and will also make it more difficult to carry your pet to the car if you need to transport them. For that reason, you have about 90 minutes with your Dear Dog before it's time to take them to be cremated/buried. (Unless you're at a clinic, at which point you may be given less time. Ask in advance if this is important to you.)

- ♥ If you had your dog euthanized someplace other than home, have a friend or family member come with you. Driving afterward can be difficult when you feel emotionally distraught.

There are three options of where to euthanize your Dear Dog:

AT YOUR HOME

Being at home may be less stressful for your furbaby, especially if they are usually nervous or scared at the vet's or hate riding in the car. Being in familiar surroundings can be comforting for you, too. However, some Dog Parents prefer not to have these kinds of sad memories associated with an area in their house.

If you opt for an at-home euthanasia, your current vet may provide this service. If not, you can contact a mobile vet. Ask your current vet for a recommendation or search online for "mobile vet euthanasia" and your city.

AT A VET CLINIC OR HOSPITAL

If you have a good relationship with your current vet, you may prefer they perform this final act of compassion for your Dear Dog. They can take care of all the details — all you need to do is make the appointment. Or, if you're in an after-hours emergency situation, you may have no choice but to have an emergency hospital veterinarian euthanize your pet.

Either vet will have the expertise and facilities to handle your dog's euthanasia process from start to finish, including transporting your dog's body to a pet cemetery/crematory. Having a vet euthanize your furbaby in-clinic can cost less than at home, while an after-hours euthanasia at an emergency vet hospital can be the most expensive.

AT AN ANIMAL SHELTER'S VET CLINIC

Some animal shelters offer low-cost veterinary services to the community. In addition to spaying/neutering they may also provide owner-requested humane euthanasia. Most will not allow you to be in the room during the euthanasia, but may give you time with your pet afterward.

Do What's Best for You

This is a very personal decision and ultimately you need to do what is best for you. We suggest you start by talking with your current vet. Bring the "Euthanasia Services with My Vet" Guide Sheet #12 on page 116 with you to that appointment to gather information. You can use a copy of the same guide sheet when talking to a mobile vet.

FILL OUT

Euthanasia Services on page 116

WEBSITE:
GoodbyeDearDog.com/guidesheets

3. Decide How To Handle Remains

The next decision you need to make is how you want to handle your Dear Dog's body after euthanasia.

CREMATION

♥ **Private (individual):** Your pet would be cremated alone and his ashes given to you. Some people like to keep their pet's ashes in a special urn at home, or bury/scatter them somewhere special such as a garden at the pet cemetery or favorite place in nature.

If there isn't a pet cemetery in your area, consider a pet cemetery elsewhere such as Best Friends Pet Memorial Garden in southern Utah.

♥ **Communal (group):** Your pet would be cremated with several other pets, and then their ashes spread around a section of the pet cemetery. Some people like having a special place to visit and remember their pet. Being in this setting, surrounded by all the loving pet memorials can be healing. This option is less expensive than private cremation.

After an at-home euthanasia, some pet crematories can pick up your pet from home if you make arrangements in advance. Pet crematories may include your pet's paw print and fur clipping as keepsakes for an additional cost.

If you ask the euthanizing vet to handle your pet's cremation, they will place the body in a plastic bag and store in a special freezer until transporting your dog to the pet crematory — usually later that day or the next business day.

BURIAL

♥ **Home:** If you live rurally, or if your city's ordinances allow it, you may opt to bury your dog on your property. Be sure to bury your pet four or more feet deep. Mark the grave with a special plaque or other meaningful sign. Ask the euthanizing vet to place your pet in a special cardboard casket or biodegradable burial box.

♥ **Pet Cemetery:** If you decide to have your pet buried at your local pet cemetery, you can select a casket and headstone. Sometimes funeral services are available, or you may conduct your own memorial service.

Now that you've made decisions for your pet's euthanasia and cremation or burial, gather all the info together in one place on Guide Sheet #13 on page 117.

We'll explore who to turn to for support in a moment.

FILL OUT
End-of-Life Plan on page 117

WEBSITE:
GoodbyeDearDog.com/ guidesheets

4. Accept Events May Not Go As Planned

Getting everything you wrote down on Guide Sheet #13 might not be possible when the time comes. Life is full of circumstances beyond our control.

For example, if your furkid needs to be euthanized after-hours in an emergency situation, you may not be able to take her body with you. Or, depending on where you live, not all of the options discussed in this section might be available to you like a pet cemetery.

Sometimes we cannot give our Dear Dogs a peaceful passing. For instance, you might be on your way to the emergency hospital — like Marisa was with her Chihuahua Lou —when your dog dies.

Or like Marilyn had to do with her Border Collie Gracie, you might be forced to choose euthanasia in a moment of crisis.

Here are several other real-life scenarios where you might need to make a quick decision for euthanasia:

- ♥ Your dog is hit by a car, and requires complicated life-saving surgery that costs far more than you can afford.
- ♥ Your dog goes in for surgery to remove a tumor in her abdomen and the vet discovers inoperable cancer everywhere.
- ♥ You live rurally and the closest specialist who could save your dog's life is five hours away, and it's unlikely your dog will survive that long.

EMERGENCY PREPARATION

Take these steps now just in case you find yourself in an emergency situation:

1. Find out where the nearest after-hours/emergency pet hospital is.
2. Put the emergency hospital address and contact information into your phone as "VET-EMERGENCY."
3. Write the info on a piece of paper and put on your fridge.
4. Add it to your Dear Dog Binder if you have one (see page 9).
5. Be sure your dog sitter has this info as well.

Remember, if you don't get exactly what you had planned for in your Dear Dog's End-of-Life Plan, you did the best you could with circumstances outside your control.

EMERGENCY!

Prepare for emergency situations now — just in case. Find the nearest emergency vet hospital and save the info in your phone.

5. Seek Support Before and After

For many of us losing our canine companion is as painful as losing a human family member. In his article, "When my dog died, I didn't understand why it felt like a human had died," Alvin Chang explores why.

Research shows dogs offer more support than people offer to each other. Dogs give us reliable relationships. They let us take care of them. They are there for us through the ups and downs of life. They provide unconditional love.

Relationships with humans, on the other hand, are more uncertain and complex.

As Alvin says, "The symbiotic relationship [between dog and human] has evolved; we don't hunt together anymore, but we still help each other survive."

> "No one ever tells you that when your dog is dying, it feels like a human is dying."
>
> —Alvin Chang, Rainbow's Dad

I definitely felt that way with Kali. Without her, would I survive? I'm grateful for Alvin's article for helping me understand that it is normal to grieve the loss of my dog as deeply as I would a human being. You can read his article at the link in the "Read More" box.

READ MORE

Alvin Chang's Article

WEBSITE: GoodbyeDearDog.com/resources

Adobe Stock Image

Don't Be Afraid to Ask for Help

Because losing our beloved dog is as painful as losing any other family member, it is important to seek support before, during and after euthanizing your pet.

GET SUPPORT

Pet Loss Support Groups & Resources

WEBSITE: GoodbyeDearDog.com/resources

BEFOREHAND

Here are some ideas of who to reach out to before your Dear Dog's death:

- ♥ Ask **a trusted friend or family member** to come with you to your Dear Dog's euthanasia.

- ♥ Ask that **same friend or family member** if they could drive. It can be difficult to drive yourself after your pet's death.

- ♥ Tell **your boss** that you will be taking the day off if that is the case (highly recommended). If you cannot do that and need to go in to work, plan on leaving work early — do not try to go back to work afterward.

- ♥ Let **your children's teachers** know what is happening so they can be extra kind and respond with understanding to any unusual behaviors.

AFTERWARD

Here are some suggestions of where to turn after your Dear Dog's death:

- ♥ **Trusted friends and family members**

- ♥ **In-person pet bereavement support groups**
  — Search online or call your local human hospice organization for suggestions.

- ♥ **Online pet bereavement support groups**
  — Search online, or check out the list of pet loss support groups and resources on our website. See the link in the "Get Support" box.

- ♥ **Our Goodbye Dear Dog support group**
  — Join our Facebook support group at GoodbyeDearDog.com/support

Support groups — whether online or in-person — help us feel less alone in our grief. Being surrounded by people who understand what we are going through, a place where we can express our feelings without judgment, can be very healing. Also, support groups give us a chance to offer solace to others.

When you feel sad or lonely, who will you turn to in your moment of grief? Add those people to the bottom of Guide Sheet #13 on page 117. This is such a kindness to your future self.

SAY MANTRA

Put your hands over your heart and say aloud:

"When I listen to my heart, I do good things."

"My heart is bigger than my hurt."

6. Trust Yourself and Your Decision

If you chose euthanasia after listening to both your head and your heart, you have done the best you possibly can for your pup. Your Dear Dog couldn't ask any more of you than that.

Now that your decision is made, and the arrangements are in place, it's time to trust yourself.

♥ No more second-guessing.
♥ No more searching for miracle options.
♥ No more "what if's."

Instead …. repeat our Mantra and Affirmation:

*"When I listen to my heart, I do good things.
My heart is bigger than my hurt."*

Raúl Martínez's dog, Mina, brings his family lots of joy — just don't leave your food unattended!

Trusting Our Decision to Let Kali Go

When we made the decision to euthanize Kali, I pulled out my sketchbook and let myself just draw whatever came to mind.

I'd look over at her and a memory or thought would pop into my mind, and I'd try to capture it. I'm not visually artistic and it doesn't matter — that wasn't the point.

To me, the drawing represents a dumbbell toy she loved, ocean waves from the beach where she loved to play fetch, and a trail from one of our many happy hikes together.

I found it comforting to do this. It also helped me accept our decision to euthanize her.

I still have the drawing and look at it from time to time. I put it into Kali's memory book.

Help yourself make peace with your decision the way I did with Kali by filling out Guide Sheet #14. It can be very healing to do something so tactile and right-brained after you've been doing so much worrying and thinking. Think of it as art therapy!

Encourage other family members to draw their own pictures too — especially children. You could even sit down together as a family and draw your pictures at the same time. What a wonderful way to remember your special pet.

FILL OUT

Trusting My Decision on page 118

WEBSITE:
GoodbyeDearDog.com/guidesheets

GUIDE SHEET #12

DOG'S NAME: _____ TODAY'S DATE: _____

Euthanasia Services with My Vet or A Mobile Vet

INSTRUCTIONS: You may have already talked to your vet about this — **look back at Guide Sheet #1, question 5** to see what s/he said. If not, bring this guide sheet to your next vet appointment to discuss with the doc. Or call the clinic and talk with the receptionist. (Use a copy of this guide sheet if you talk to a mobile vet about in-home euthanasia.)

1. **How does your euthanasia procedure work? Do you use the single- or two-injection process?**
   _____
   _____
   _____

2. **How much time will I have with my dog afterward?** _____
   _____
   _____

3. **Do you offer at-home euthanasia?**   ☐ Yes   ☐ No
   a. If yes, what are the costs for an in-clinic euthanasia versus at my home? _____
      _____
      _____
   b. If no, who do you recommend? _____
      _____
      _____

4. **Do you handle cremation and transportation?**   ☐ Yes   ☐ No
   a. If yes, how much will that cost? _____
      _____
   b. If no, who do you recommend? _____
      _____
      _____

5. **Any other questions you have for your vet regarding euthanasia services:**
   _____
   _____
   _____
   _____
   _____
   _____
   _____
   _____

©2020 Dorothea Deley. www.GoodbyeDearDog.com

GUIDE SHEET #13

DOG'S NAME: _____   TODAY'S DATE: _____

End-of-Life Plan for My Dear Dog

INSTRUCTIONS: Review Guide Sheet #12. Mark the end-of-life services you have selected from the options below. Then fill out the rest of the checklist on this guide sheet.

Who will euthanize my Dear Dog?

☐ **MY VET**
Vet's Name: _____
Vet's Phone: _____

☐ **MOBILE/OTHER VET**
Vet's Name: _____
Vet's Phone: _____

Where will my Dear Dog be euthanized?

☐ **AT VET'S OFFICE**
Clinic Name: _____
Address: _____
_____

☐ **AT MY HOME**

When will my Dear Dog be euthanized?

Date: _____   Time: _____

What will happen to my Dear Dog's body afterward?

☐ **CREMATION**
Crematory Name: _____
Phone: _____
Address: _____
_____

☐ **BURIAL**
Cemetery (if applicable): _____
Phone: _____
Address: _____
_____

Private Cremation:	**Group Cremation:**	**Bury at Home:**	**Bury at Pet Cemetery:**
☐ I want ashes back	☐ I do not want ashes back (crematory staff can scatter ashes at pet cemetery)	☐ I checked my city/county ordinances and it is legal for me to bury my pet on my property.	☐ I want my pet buried in his own plot with a headstone or memorial plaque
☐ I want ashes buried or inurned in mausoleum or niche at pet cemetery			

How will my Dear Dog's remains be transported for burial/cremation?

☐ **VET WILL TRANSPORT**   ☐ **I WILL TRANSPORT**   ☐ **PET CEMETERY WILL TRANSPORT**

Who will I turn to for support before and after?

☐ **FRIENDS & FAMILY MEMBERS**
Names & Phone #s: _____
_____
_____
_____

Who from the above list will be with me during my Dear Dog's euthanasia? _____

☐ **PET LOSS SUPPORT GROUPS**
In-person Location & Meeting Times:
_____
_____
_____

Website & Meeting Times:
_____
_____
_____

©2020 Dorothea Deley. www.GoodbyeDearDog.com

GUIDE SHEET #14

DOG'S NAME: _____ TODAY'S DATE: _____

Trusting My Decision

INSTRUCTIONS: Grab some markers, paints, colored pencils, crayons, or just pick up a pen. Then, take a moment to look at or think about your Dear Dog. Draw or color whatever comes up for you in the space below (or on your own paper). It could be abstract splashes of color or a literal rendering of your dog — anything you create is perfect.

KALI'S STORY

Goodbye Dear Kali

We wanted to say goodbye to Kali at home, so Mike found a mobile vet who would come to our house. She reminded us of our rural vet back in Colorado.

Mike prepared a pallet of blankets in our living room for Kali to lie on. He surrounded it with her favorite toys.

When Dr. Blanche walked in, she immediately went to Kali. She sat on the floor next to her and gently stroked her. "Tell me more about Kali's symptoms," she said.

We told her about the fainting and the weekly trips to the vet to drain the fluid from her abdomen. We listed her medications, which seemed to make her feel worse. We admitted Kali didn't move much anymore and lately had to be hand-fed.

"See how Kali just lays here," Dr Blanche said, "how she didn't even look at me when I first walked in?" We nodded our heads yes. "But your other dog, Jenna, is curious, right? She showed interest in me, she wanted to know who is this stranger coming into her home?"

Dr. Blanche turned back to Kali and said, "Do you see how Kali can barely hold her head up? That's because holding her head up puts pressure on her windpipe because of the edema, and that makes it harder to breathe." She patted Kali. "That's no way to live. This poor baby is hurting."

Dr. Blanche looked up at me. "I need you to not cry right now," she said. "Kali needs you to be strong so she's not scared, okay?" I blinked back the tears and whispered, "Okay."

Giving Kali Her Last Command

While Dr. Blanche prepared the syringes, Mike and I sat on either side of the pallet. Kali was lying in the hallway watching us. "It's time," Dr. Blanche said.

Mike and I gave Kali the hand signal for "Come."

Kali struggled to get herself up, and then slowly walked toward us. Mike patted the yellow blanket for her to lie on. She gingerly eased her swollen body down and eyed the bowl of liver near the vet.

Mike and I looked at each other with tears in our eyes. We had just given our Baby Bups the very last command of her life.

KALI'S STORY, continued

While we fed Kali the liver to distract her, Dr. Blanche gave Kali the first injection of sedative in her rump. A moment later Kali fell asleep. Then the vet shaved Kali's foreleg, swabbed it with alcohol and found a vein. She explained the next injection would stop Kali's heart.

For a split second my brain screamed, "NO! Please don't give her the second shot. Please." But I didn't say anything. I just petted my dog.

Dr. Blanche gave Kali the second injection. Kali's breathing slowed, and then stopped. She lost a little urine. I felt her body cool beneath my hand. The vet put on her stethoscope and listened for Kali's heartbeat for a minute. Then she looked up at us and quietly said, "She's gone."

Driving Kali to the Cemetery

Once Kali was gone and Dr. Blanche had left, we had about an hour before we needed to drive Kali to the pet crematory.

I knelt beside Kali and petted her soft fur. I told her how much I loved her. I shared some of my favorite memories of her.

Then we lifted Kali's body, using her blanket like a stretcher the way Dr. Blanche had instructed us. We carried her out to the car for her last ride.

When we walked into the pet crematory office, the receptionist warmly welcomed us. "I can have José get Kali out of your car if you'd like," she said.

While Mike answered her questions, I watched as José gently loaded Kali into a little wagon.

Yes, we wanted her cremated with her blanket.

Yes, we wanted her cremated alone and we wanted her ashes back.

No, we did not want to purchase an urn.

Yes, we would like a fur clipping and paw print keepsake.

José pulled the wagon across the parking lot and paused at the office doorway. I looked at my Dear Dog for the last time, and whispered, "Goodbye Kali. I love you."

SECTION SIX:
Talking to Your Kids

> "Children have their own special relationships with their pets. ... It's important to help prepare children for the loss of your family's companion animal."
>
> — *Argus Institute at Colorado State University Veterinary Teaching Hospital,* Making Decisions When Your Companion Animal is Sick

Supporting children through the goodbye process

THE STORY OF MOJITO & MADDY

Remember Nicöle Beer and her Chihuahua from page 96? When Nicöle decided to euthanize Mojito, she had to explain why to her then 4-year-old daughter, Maddy.

First she explained that as Mojito's owners, it was their job to make sure he lived a life free from pain. "Then I told her that we could try to do more to help him live a little bit longer," says Nicöle, "but he would be scared, confused and in a lot of pain for the extra little bit of life we could give him. So that evening after Maddy went to bed, the vet would come to the house and give Mojito a shot to make him die."

At the time Maddy seemed to understand why her parents chose euthanasia. But for the next year-and-a-half she would occasionally ask why they decided to "kill" Mojito instead of save him.

"Sometimes Maddy would tell us that if it was her choice she would have decided to save Mojito," Nicöle says. "I think, at 4, Maddy had a hard time grasping why we could have extended his life but chose not to. In retrospect I wish I had not explained the two options to her, and only explained the part about ending his pain and suffering."

Maddy decided that cremating Mojito and keeping his ashes at home would be best because he always liked being at home. They also made a memory book filled with photos of "Momo."

Sometimes Nicöle would find Maddy sitting on her bed, looking through the memory book. "She'd say that our doggie Mojito can still be alive in our imagination and dreams," Nicöle says. "I told her that's exactly how we keep the people we love alive in our hearts after they die."

Now eight years old, Maddy still talks about Mojito. Just the other day Nicöle overheard Maddy say to their new dog, "George, you and Mojito would have been such good friends!"

After 4-year-old Maddy's dog, Mojito, died, she continued to draw pictures and write stories about him at school for the next year and a half.

Children's Special Relationship with Dogs

Your Dear Dog may be your child's best friend.

Someone to talk to when they're lonely. Someone to hug when they're scared. Someone to play with outside on sunny days or laugh with inside on rainy ones.

Someone who is always happy to see them, no matter what. Someone who never scolds or tells them to do their homework. Someone who loves them for who they are, and thinks they are the BEST. THING. EVER!

Every child could use a friend like that.

For many kids, losing a pet may be their first experience with death. That's why it's so important to spend time talking with your children beforehand, explaining your decision to euthanize their buddy in age-appropriate language, giving them a chance to say goodbye if possible, and then helping them grieve afterward.

We'll explore how to support your child in the next few pages.

WATCH THIS

Maddy Plays with Mojito

WEBSITE: GoodbyeDearDog.com/videos

> "We need to give our children permission to express themselves and work through their grief — not bury it."
>
> — *Dr. Ron Hines, Second Chance Animal Sanctuary*

WATCH THIS

How Vicky Talked with Her Kids

WEBSITE: GoodbyeDearDog.com/videos

Explaining Euthanasia to Your Child

Deciding what to tell your child very much depends on their age.

Four-year-old Maddy's misunderstanding of euthanasia as a loving choice is natural for a child her age. Abstract concepts like suffering and compassion — key factors in most decisions to euthanize — are difficult to explain to a young child.

Vicky Rees' sons, on the other hand, ranged in age from 10-14 when the family decided to euthanize their beloved Jake. She and her husband explained the euthanasia process to the boys, and asked if they'd like to be present. "Even though that's a really difficult experience for a young person to have," Vicky says. "We felt they were old enough to be able to make that choice."

All three boys wanted to go, so the next morning the family went to the vet's together You can hear more about their experience at the link in the "Watch This" box.

Here are suggestions for how to talk to your child about euthanasia according to the Association of Pet Loss and Bereavement and the Argus Institute at Colorado State University:

Be honest, and use direct and clear language.

- ♥ While your instinct might be to protect your child by using softer phrases like "put to sleep," it's best to be direct. Younger children especially can be scared and confused by those kinds of euphemisms. Since they "go to sleep" every night, they may worry about never waking up.

- ♥ Explain in age-appropriate words what euthanasia is and how it works. A very young child may only understand euthanasia in the simplest terms, such as: "Spot is ready to die now. The doggie doctor will help Spot die with special medicine. Spot won't feel anything."

- ♥ An older child might need more context, such as: "Spot is very sick. The vet tried to make him better but nothing worked. Spot hurts so much right now. We love him very much and we don't want him to be in pain. We are going to help him die now so he doesn't have to hurt anymore. Does that make sense? Do you have any questions?"

Give them a chance to say goodbye.

- ♥ Kids need to say goodbye to their best friend. Talk to your child to find out what special way they would like to do this. Perhaps you could create a goodbye ceremony together, or spend a few hours doing some of your pet's favorite activities (modified as needed). Your child may have ideas, too, so be sure to ask and honor their suggestions.

♥ If you had to euthanize your beloved dog in an emergency situation and there wasn't time to say goodbye, help your child create a special goodbye ceremony for closure.

Helping Your Child Grieve

Here are suggestions — also from the Argus Institute at Colorado State University and the Association of Pet Loss and Bereavement — for ways to support your child through the grieving process:

Ask if they'd like to plan a funeral or memorial service.

♥ After your dog's death, let your child plan a special funeral or memorial service if they want. Perhaps they'd like to invite grandparents or friends over to help them say goodbye. Or maybe they want to read a poem or letter they wrote to their dog, sing a song, pray, or tell a story.

♥ Share your beliefs about what happens after death if your child asks. Incorporate family beliefs and traditions into your pet's service if your child requests.

> "As for what happens after death, I believe that's best discussed in light of each family's traditions and beliefs. Those traditions and beliefs are important things to share with your children if and when they ask!"
>
> — *Fred Rogers, star of* Mister Rogers' Neighborhood *and author of* When A Pet Dies

Reassure them.

♥ Sometimes after a loss, kids worry about someone else close to them dying. It's important to reassure them now to ease their fears.

♥ It's also important to make it clear it's okay for them to talk about their sad feelings. If they'd rather not talk (or are too young to express feelings verbally) ask them if they'd like to make some art about how they feel.

Share your feelings.

♥ It's okay for your child to see you cry or be sad before, during and after your dog's euthanasia. Seeing you express your feelings may help them express their own, which is an important part of the grieving process.

♥ Healthy grieving now helps children practice coping skills they'll need to deal with loss later in life.

WATCH THIS

Marisa Describes Memorial Ceremony with Godkids

WEBSITE: GoodbyeDearDog.com/videos

SECTION SIX: TALKING TO YOUR KIDS

Keep to your usual family schedule.

♥ Losing a dog upsets our daily routine — no matter our age. Maybe one of your child's chores was to feed your dog. Or maybe as a family you went to the doggie park on Sunday afternoons. Obviously some of your schedule must change now. But any part of your regular schedule that you can maintain after your dog dies will give your child a sense of stability.

Make a memorial corner in your house.

♥ Help your child pick out a special place in your home to set up a memorial for your dog. Perhaps on top of the mantle, on a bookshelf, or a hanging photo mobile. You could even set up a little table. Wherever you set up a memorial, place your dog's photo and other keepsakes like a favorite toy or collar there. This is a nice place for your Dear Dog's ashes too, if you'd like.

♥ Setting up a memorial shows your child that your Dear Dog is a beloved family member and death does not stop that from being true. It can be frightening to a child to see you getting rid of Spot's food bowl, toys, leash, and bed. A visible memorial reassures your child that it is okay to talk about your dog, remembering fun times together as well as sharing sad feelings when they come up.

Photo by Dorothea Deley

On Kali's memorial table we placed her photo, paw print, fur clippings, collar and ashes. The rock is from her favorite beach, where she spent hours chasing her favorite toy, that orange dumbbell. Above the table we hung a photo mobile of some of our favorite pictures of her, including a silly one of her and Mike hugging in their sleep!

Read books with them about pet loss and grief.
- ♥ There are many children's books about death and dying, grief, and pet loss. We suggest *When A Pet Dies* by Fred Rogers. See the link in the "Read More" box.
- ♥ Take your child to your local library or bookstore and spend some time looking at books together. Let your child select one or two books to take home.

Give them time to grieve before adopting another pet.
- ♥ Let your children process their grief before adopting a new dog. A new dog cannot replace their best friend, and it's best to wait until your child has had enough time to understand and accept that their dog is not coming back before you bring in another family member.

READ MORE

Children's Book
When a Pet Dies
by Fred Rogers

WEBSITE:
GoodbyeDearDog.com/
resources

Be Extra Kind to Your Kids

Loss is such a natural part of life. Helping your child grieve in a healthy way can help them grow into more resilient adults.

For now, just know your child will need extra:

- ♥ love, support, patience and kindness
- ♥ understanding that losing their best buddy is a significant loss
- ♥ opportunities to talk about their feelings and how much they miss their pet, or to tell funny stories they remember spontaneously
- ♥ hugs!

> "When [my childhood dog] Mitzi died I was very sad, and so were my parents. We had lost a member of the family. My parents encouraged me to talk about how I felt, and they let me know that grieving was a natural, healing thing to do."
>
> — *Fred Rogers, from his children's book,* When A Pet Dies

Notes and Ideas

SECTION SEVEN:
Resources to Support You

" Clementine was the kind of soul that transcended 'pet.' Reflecting on her nature makes me want to be a better human being. ...The world needs more Clementines."

— *Stu Carlson, Clementine's Dad*

Photo by Stu Carlson

POEM FOR CLEMENTINE

Today we say goodbye to our Clementine.

Protector of girls, giver of kisses, constant companion and faithful friend to the end.

She never knew a stranger, or a dark thought, or the boundary of a fence. She roamed far, always returning to watch over us. She was truly one of a kind.

We are so lucky to have known you. Thank you for teaching us and loving us.

Roam In Peace sweet Clementine.

We miss you and will love you always.

— *Stu Carlson, Clementine's Dad*

Recommendations For Online Researching

The Internet offers a plethora of information — sometimes useful, sometimes confusing, almost always overwhelming.

Getting sucked into an Internet black hole will not help you or your dog. In fact, it may be a way to distract yourself from the painful situation with your pup. Or a way to give you a sense of control when you feel helpless. Or maybe a way to numb out from what's really going on around you.

For these reasons, we recommend you:

♥ **Limit your research to just a few trusted veterinary websites.**
  – See our suggested "Trusted Vet Sites" on the next page.

♥ **Time-box your time spent online.**
  – Set a timer for 15 to 60 minutes and when it goes off, move away from the computer.
  – Take days off! Designate one or two days a week as your "Tech Sabbath." Spend some time outside in the fresh air or doing something you enjoy instead of sitting at the computer.

♥ **Avoid researching at night.**
  – Shut down your computer at least an hour before bedtime to help your mind unwind and relax.
  – Skip logging on if you wake up in the middle of the night with a burning urge to look up something online.
  – Accept that staying up all night — or getting up in the middle of the night when you can't sleep — won't magically yield new answers you missed during the day.
  – Understand that your Dear Dog needs you well-rested right now. You'll be a better caregiver and decision maker if you're strong and energetic.

Trusted Veterinary Websites

Veterinarians have years of training and real-life experience that we cannot replicate with a web search. While I can't stop you from playing "Google Vet" and doing your own research, I encourage you to stick to reputable sites. Below are several veterinarian sites I found particularly helpful when Kali was sick. (See the "Read More" box for direct links.)

READ MORE

Trusted Vet Sites

WEBSITE: GoodbyeDearDog.com/resources

Lap of Love Veterinary Hospice

Drs. Dani McVety and Mary Gardner run a pet hospice clinic in Florida and manage a nationwide network of mobile hospice and euthanasia veterinarians. Check out their "Educational Pet Disease Series" for basic information about your Dear Dog's illness

Second Chance Animal Sanctuary

Dr. Ron Hines explains clearly the most common diseases he treats at his clinic in Texas. He includes diagrams and information about how the diseases might progress. I found his site invaluable for understanding Kali's congestive heart failure. (Scroll down to the "Dog" section.)

Argus Foundation at Colorado State University

Since 1984, the Argus Institute Counseling and Support Services at Colorado State's vet school has helped families make hospice arrangements for their ill pets, and supported them through the euthanasia process with online and in-person resources. You might want to order the "Making Decisions When Your Companion Animal is Sick" booklet, too.

Dr. Alice Villalobos's Pawspice for Cancer Care

If your Dear Dog suffers from cancer, Dr. Alice Villalobos specializes in end-of-life oncology care. She also writes about quality of life, euthanasia decisions and grieving.

Dr. Patty Khuly's articles on PetMD

Like WebMD for people, PetMD explores animal illnesses from symptoms to treatments. We found Dr. Patty Khuly's articles especially useful.

Dog Dementia Help & Support

Eileen Anderson created this thoughtful website after her Dear Dog, Cricket, was diagnosed with Canine Cognitive Dysfunction (doggie dementia). We had no idea such a thing even existed until our dog Jenna started acting "strange" after her stroke. Luckily we found Eileen's site to help us navigate Jenna's illness.

Ways We Can Support You

We put together more resources online to support you. Please visit GoodbyeDearDog.com for the following:

Download 10 Questions & All Guide Sheets

- ♥ Download all the guide sheets in one printer-friendly PDF at GoodbyeDearDog.com/guidesheets. (After printing, don't forget to put them in your Dear Dog binder!)
- ♥ You can also access all the articles, audios, videos and other resources referenced in this guidebook.

Prepare for Euthanasia

- ♥ 5 Things We Wish We'd Done Differently Before Euthanizing Kali
- ♥ 5 Things We Did Right for Our Dear Dog Kali's Euthanasia
- ♥ Making Euthanasia Arrangements
- ♥ Understanding the Euthanasia Procedure and What to Expect – Our Experience Euthanizing Kali
- ♥ Spending a Special Last Day with Your Dear Dog – Photos from Our Last Day with Kali

Memorialize Your Dear Dog

- ♥ Planning a Memorial Service – Photos from Our Memorial Service for Kali at Her Favorite Place
- ♥ Making a Photo Timeline of Your Dear Dog's Life
- ♥ Making a Memory Book
- ♥ Setting Up a Special Memorial Space in Your Home – Our Altar for Kali
- ♥ Making a Fur Pet of Your Pup
- ♥ Pet Portraits by Our Friend Vicky Rees
- ♥ Wooden Urn Boxes by Our Friend Tom Beach
- ♥ Custom Pet Charm Jewelry by Our Friend Michelle Riley

Photo by Vicky Rees

Artist Vicky Rees paints wonderful pet portraits like this one and the one of Kali on the cover. More info at www.victoriarees.com

Grieve After Your Dear Dog's Death

- ♥ Grief and What to Expect the First Year
  – Our First Year without Kali: An Audio Journal of How Our Grief Evolved over Time

- ♥ Pet Loss Support Groups and Hotlines: In-Person, Online, Phone

- ♥ Recommended Books for Coping with Pet Loss and Grief

- ♥ Virtual Remembrance Events

- ♥ Art Therapy Workshops to Help You Grieve and Memorialize Your Dear Dog

Get Support

- ♥ Sign Up for Our Email "Care Package" Before Your Dear Dog's Euthanasia and Receive:
  – A Love Note on the Day of Your Pet's Euthanasia
  – Supportive Emails Everyday for the First Week Like A Hug in Your Inbox

- ♥ Talk to Fellow Dog Parents in Our Facebook Support Group
  – Receive Support from People Who Understand
  – Read about Other People's Experiences
  – Ask Questions
  – Offer Solace to Other Dog Parents (sometimes we help ourselves most when we help someone else)
  – Share Your Own Experiences with Your Dear Dog

Benefit From Other Dog Parents' Experiences

- ♥ Watch or Read Full Interviews from Dog Parents Featured in This Guidebook

READ MORE

Grief Support & Other Helpful Resources

WEBSITE: GoodbyeDearDog.com/resources

GET SUPPORT

Email Care Package

WEBSITE:
*GoodbyeDearDog.com/
support*

The First Week is the Hardest — Let Us Help

The first week after Kali's death was by far the hardest for Mike and me.

We imagine it will be for you, too.

Please let us support you through those first few difficult days. We'd love to send you an email "Care Package"— one email a day for seven days. Think of it as a hug in your inbox.

To sign up, fill out the form on our website (see link in the "Get Support" box).

All we need is:

- ♥ your Dear Dog's name,
- ♥ the date you'll be euthanizing him/her,
- ♥ your first name, and
- ♥ email address.

We will take it from there.

"[A] teaching of sadness is compassion for others who are in pain, because it is only in feeling our own pain that we can really understand and allow for someone else's."

— *Madisyn Taylor, DailyOm.com cofounder*

CONCLUSION:
Thank You & A Gift

" In the last 48 hours since we euthanized Kali, a wave of grief hits me whenever I sense her absence. Sometimes I break down and cry. I'm trying to just feel these waves when they come and not resist them."

— *Mike Maxwell, Kali's Dad, from our "First Year Without Kali Audio Journal"*

LISTEN UP

Our First Year Without Kali

WEBSITE:
GoodbyeDearDog.com/gift

A Thank You Gift

Thank you for letting us support you on this difficult journey. It's been such a gift to honor Kali's memory this way.

Our Gift to You

Mike and I kept an audio diary for the first year after losing Kali. During that year, everything was a "first" without her — our first Christmas without her …. our first camping trip without her … our first Mother's and Father's Days.

We recorded our feelings every couple of days for the first week, and then roughly once every few months for the rest of the year.

While we can't promise your experience will be the same, it might be helpful to see how our grief evolved over time. To see how we handled grief — as a couple, as a man, as a woman, and as Dog Parents of our other dog Jenna, who also missed her sister.

As a thank you for reading this book, we'd like to offer the audio to you as a gift. Listen or download it at the link in the "Listen Up" box.

Photo by Dorothea Deley

For the first three months after Kali died, Jenna would watch the front door, waiting for Kali to come home.

Please Send Us Feedback

We want to make this guidebook as helpful as possible for Dog Parents. It would mean the world to us to hear your feedback. Please let us know:

- ♥ What about the guidebook helped you the most?
- ♥ Which of the 10 questions were most useful?
- ♥ Any suggestions you have for improving the guide sheets?

Do you have a story about saying goodbye that you'd like to share? We would love to hear from you.

See the link in the "Fill Out" box for an online form to share your feedback and stories with us.

FILL OUT

Send Us Feedback & Your Stories

WEBSITE:
GoodbyeDearDog.com/contact

Share this Guidebook with Others

Mike and I hope you found our guidebook helpful. If you have a friend or family member with a dog, please consider sharing a copy of this guidebook with them.

New Dog Parents especially may not know what to expect as their Dear Dog ages or faces an illness. Having this resource now may help them prepare to one day say goodbye.

Your Love Will Guide You

Remember ... Your heart is bigger than your hurt.

Because of your love, you will do the right thing at the right time for your Dear Dog.

Photo by Dorothea Deley

A few months after Kali's death, Mike and I took a road trip back to her favorite beach. We brought along her favorite toy and threw it in the waves 16 times — one for every year of her life.

In the midst of us throwing the toy, a woman walked by with an Australian cattle dog that looked a lot like Kali. It felt as if Kali were there with us in spirit and wanted us to know everything was okay.

That is a fitting final memory to have of my ever-independent, super smart, playful cattle dog ... my Baby Bups.

May she ever run free on her favorite beach. ♥

Acknowledgments

So many wonderful people helped bring this guidebook to life, from Dog Parents who bravely shared their stories to friends who generously gave their time and professional talents.

Heartfelt gratitude to the following people — your love for Dear Dogs affirms my faith in humanity!

Moral Support

Mike Maxwell, Vicky Rees, Marisa Waddell & Danielle Kemper MSW, LCSW for helping me through Kali's death, and supporting me through reliving that loss again and again while working on this guidebook.

Illustrations & Graphic Design

Vicky Rees, Artist / Illustrator / Graphic Designer
https://www.victoriarees.com

Editing & Book Coaching

Charmin Dahl, Coaching / Curation / Curriculum Development
https://makersearth.com

Life & Leadership Coaching

Laura W. Miner, Leadership Coach / Consultant / Author
https://www.laurawminer.com

Business Coaching

Paul Lirette, Executive Director / Executive Coach
https://SamuraiSuccess.com

Dog Parents Who Shared Their Stories

Janet Amador	Danielle Kemper	Vicky Rees
Nicöle Beer	Rachel Mendoza	Margie Rensky
Gustavo Brett	Gingy Molacek	Cindy Smith
Marilyn Colter	Craig Nuttycombe	John Thompson
Charmin Dahl	Tony Perrotti	Marisa Waddell

Readers of the First Draft Who Offered Suggestions

Andrew Adleman	Dairine Dear	Teresa Petterson, DVM
Janet Amador	Jan Jervis	Vicky Rees
Nicöle Beer	JoAnn Kalenak	Jan Simmons
Marla Carlson	Jasmine Kojouri	John Thompson
Marilyn Colter	Karla Lewis	Marisa Waddell
Steve Colter, DVM	Paul Lirette	Kay Wood
Kristin Cooper	Julie Buffa Owen	Laura Lee Yates

www.ingramcontent.com/pod-product-compliance
Lightning Source LLC
Chambersburg PA
CBHW051611030426
42334CB00035B/3489